Start Winning With Money

I0488989

Your Guide to Personal Finance, Small Business Growth, and Building Wealth

Donnie Masters

Copyright © 2017 Masters Investment Group, LLC

All rights reserved.

Without limiting the rights under copyright reserved above, no part of this publication may be reproduced or distributed in any form or by any means, or stored in a database or retrieval system without the prior written permission of Masters Investment Group.

This book is for informational purposes only. This information is provided with the understanding that the publisher and individual writer are not engaged in rendering financial or other professional services. Past results are not necessarily an indication of future performance. The authors and publisher specifically disclaim any responsibility for any liability, loss, or risk, personal or otherwise ,incurred as a consequence, directly or indirectly, of the use and application of any contents of this book.

ISBN-13: 978-1521171165

DEDICATION

To my loving wife, Jennifer. Without you I would not be on this fantastic voyage of writing and sharing my message with the world. You give me inspiration, motivation, and a desire to win with you by my side. I love you.

For Aiden and Wyatt. Don't stop chasing your dreams for one single day! If I can do this, than you can do whatever you want in life. You both deserve greatness and I hope you get all you ever dream of.

I thank those that encourage me.
I care for those that support me.
I love those that believe in me.
I pray for those that underestimate me.

-Donnie Masters
www.donniemasters.com

CONTENTS

ACKNOWLEDGMENTS

Writing is an art form that is never done alone. Yes, the hours are spent alone at a computer writing and editing, but your family bears the brunt of the burden as you can not be with them at certain events or activities. As an author, your family must support you or the task of the writer becomes a burden on the entire family, not just the writer himself.

I am blessed to be loved by a woman that wants me to write and share my message with the world. She thinks I am pretty good at it. She will openly admit that I have changed her mind on finances and opened up a world to her that she never would have known. I hope my passion for the subject of living well and wealth shine through while you are reading this.

This book came together as many people have asked me financial questions and sought advice over the years. Some of my ideas for this book have been borrowed from those questions or conversations. There are far too many friends, colleagues, and acquaintances to count or list here by name.

I wanted to write a book that should be handed to every child that enters the workforce during the ages of 15-18. I wanted a guide that someone should have handed me all those years ago. It is not intended to be an end all, be all book about money and finance. It is intended to set the record straight before you make a lot of big money decisions. I believe this book can genuinely place someone on the right foot going forward.

I personally believe the key to true wealth is a simple formula that involves a combination of work, timing, and knowledge. No one achieves greatness without all three of these factors. Please do not confuse wealth with money. All the money in the world can not make you wealthy. Wealth can not be bought. It is achieved.

Your bank account does not dictate what you are! I know

many people that do not have more than $5,000 in their bank accounts, but are truly wealthy in life. True wealth is a combination of love, family, friends, money, and time. When you have all 5 of these things in tune with the other, true wealth has been achieved.

By the end of this book I hope you will have learned a few things that you can apply in your life to make it better. Whether you are on the road to wealth already, or need a refresher course, this book should offer you some insight into your financial future. Please join me on this journey as we walk down the road of finances, business, and ultimately building true wealth.

CHAPTER 1
YOU WERE TAUGHT TO FAIL AT FINANCE

As a small child I remember setting my dreams on being an astronaut, doctor, and a businessman. In fact, with all my youthful inexperience unchecked, I honestly believed that I could be all three at the same time! Nowhere in my childhood dreams did it ever register that I would never accomplish ANYTHING without being dedicated and committed to a chosen craft. It never once crossed my mind that there was zero chance of being a contributing member of your field when you are splitting your time between three completely different fields of study. Naive, yes, but childhood is amazing that way.

I specifically remember being formed and shaped in my early teen years by the public school system here in West Virginia. I was actually a really good student and enjoyed most of my classes and teachers, even if the particular subject was not of interest to me.

West Virginia, where I was born and raised, uses middle schools to teach grades 6, 7, and 8. This is when I remember beginning to take some of the more "unnecessary" classes. These were classes that were required to be taught at a certain period in time, but their practicality in the modern world was questionable at best.

I remember having to take a shop class where we built bridges from balsa wood, bird houses, and maybe even a cup holder if you were at an advanced level (I clearly wasn't). Kids spent hours sanding and painting their crafts. Fun for a boy of 12-14, but not practical in the real world.

Then I had Home Economics another year where we learned to sew, bake, and clean. Maybe this was practical 40 years ago when a wife stayed at home, but in today's world this was wasted time as well.

The one thing that school never bothered to teach me was that in the real world everything you need or want revolves around the almighty dollar. There truly is no such thing as a free lunch, and even the most free spirited and care-free person will need money for groceries and clothes. It's just how the real world works as an adult.

Reality began to sink in for me during my high school years. I started to work for a local sub shop at the age of 15. I remember how much fun it was to get a paycheck and have absolutely zero responsibility to that money. I could buy whatever I wanted because I had earned it. I could fulfill my immediate desires because I had cash in my pocket. I knew right then and there that I was a person motivated by money. I wanted better things in life and I had figured out the secret formula. If you make more money you can spend more money.

Sadly, I never had one single class that taught me how to do a personal budget and properly spend my money. Not one hour of one day was ever spent on balancing a checkbook or reading a bank statement. Not one teacher taught us anything about paychecks and taxes. Even worse, we were thrown out in the "real world" without any understanding of the stock market. No one spent any time advising how to pick good mutual funds as part of your 401(k). The expectation was simply for all students was to go to college and then get a "real" job that paid a livable wage. That was everyone's predetermined path, like it or not.

At this point in my adult life, I have figured out that school doesn't teach a lot of things that are needed in the real world. Financial education was by far my biggest disappointment with the school system. Not far behind that however was my disappointment with the guidance counselors. No one was ever told that there are more options than just college. If you had the grades, you were expected to go to college, plain and simple.

On another sad note, there was never a conversation had about building or creating a business from the ground up (For the record, I graduated high school in 1998, right before the dot com bubble and people were printing money just by having a dot com idea). Read the story of Pets.com if you need reminded of that crazy era.

My larger point is that a student like me was never given a chance to succeed during my younger years of life. I didn't have the contacts or support system to do it because nothing was offered, taught, or even advised. The school system failed me then and it is still failing kids now!

So after I figured out making more money made life easier, making more and more money became my new pursuit during high school. I learned pretty quickly that when I worked more hours they would pay me more money. If I could save some of that extra money, then I could buy my own car when I turned 16. I did exactly that.

My life became different the day I bought my first car. Most guys are excited to have their own wheels so they can fix it up and take out their girlfriend on Friday night. That wasn't what I was most excited about. Don't get me wrong, I was excited and I loved the ladies, but my excitement was all about my freedom. I had finally purchased a ticket to wherever I wanted to go!

My enthusiasm was quickly buffered by the big bill that my father laid in front of me the following day. I remember the conversation like it was yesterday.

"It is going to cost almost $200 per month to add you to our insurance policy. Now that you have your own car, you are responsible for that every month."

"Uh, yeah. OK. No problem, Dad."

So the first day of every month I handed my father $200 for the extra insurance premiums due on the insurance policy. This is when being a responsible adult kicked in and money began to feel less fun. It just didn't feel the same to me anymore. I still had plenty of money every week, but it felt different knowing that I had to pay that bill each and every month. I had responsibilities now and that meant financial commitments to go along with them.

I ended up getting fired after about 6 months at the local sub shop. I had turned 16 by now, and I screwed up a really good thing. I was a complete smart ass to the wrong customer. He was the owner's friend, and I took out some of my bad attitude on him. It wasn't his fault I had a bad day at school, but I let all my frustrations out on him anyway. I honestly don't even remember what had happened that day at school to set me off. I can't recall the exact conversation to the customer as I write this either. Whatever was said to him, it was more than enough reason to let me go and they did the following day.

I finished high school while working at an Italian fast food chain. I stayed for about 18 months and worked my way up from dishwasher to "Golden Tomato". In fact, I was one of only three people in the entire restaurant trained to run any position. Since this was a new concept in my hometown, I was in the first class of recipients that earned the award. I thought that I was special.

When one was granted "Golden Tomato" status, they were supposed to receive a pay raise as an incentive for accomplishing that goal. The pay raise was an extra incentive that the company provided so that people would spend time cross-training and learning new positions. I had a meeting with the store manager the following week. I expected to hear congratulations and praise. Boy was I wrong!

"Hey Donnie. Come on in and sit down for a minute," said Ron. He continued, "You know. I was thinking about your pay raise over this past week, and I just don't see why we should give you one." I stayed silent. This was praise and congratulations? He just kept rambling on, not even really looking at me while talking. He would glance in my direction and then talk to the wall some more.

"We gave you an annual pay raise in May. Then they adjusted the minimum wage up again and we kept you way above that as well. We just can't afford to give you more at this time."

"So do you want my notice in writing or is a verbal good enough?" I responded.

"Now let's not get crazy about this or anything. We still want you to work here for us. You have put in too much time to just walk away..."

I cut him off at this point, I was fuming!

"I will hand you my notice in writing then tomorrow. Good night Ron."

I was making $5.40 per hour at the time. Minimum wage had just recently increased to $5.15 per hour, and the company agreed to keep all pay the same as before. What that meant was if you were making minimum wage you stayed there. If you had earned and extra .10 or .15 per hour, you were paid that on top of the minimum wage as before. I had been with the company for 18 months and had earned 3 separate pay raises while learning all the different positions. I was worth .25 more per hour than the other guy because I knew everything about every position.

I didn't speak to Ron the next day, he wasn't working. I handed in my 2 week notice to the manager on duty and went on about my shift. After the dinner rush had died out, Judy asked me to talk with her outside for a minute.

"Grab those trash cans and come out here with me."

I emptied the trash cans into the dumpster as she fired up her Marlboro Light 100.

"What are you going to do? Where are you going?" she asked, exhaling a cloud of smoke into the atmosphere.

"I don't know Judy, but I can tell you one thing. I am not going to stay here and work for some guy that doesn't think I earned that pay raise."

"Is that what he said to you?" she asked.

I told Judy the whole story from beginning to end, making sure to explain all the previous pay raises that were earned as well. She listened to me explain how is was explained to the employees when we first opened up.

"I was a dishwasher Judy! I worked from the bottom up to get my spot, my hours, and my money. Who does he think he is with this bullshit?"

Judy finished her cigarette and opened the door leading back into the restaurant. She followed me back inside and shut the door. That was all that was said that night. I finished my shift and went home.

Behind the scenes, Judy started lobbying for me. She began calling a lot of her former contacts and sent out feelers to her former colleagues. She had already set up an interview for me when I came back to work a couple days later.

"Donnie, I need you to listen to me," she spoke softly. "I got an opportunity for a good worker like you."

"Judy that's awesome! When and where do I need to go?"

Judy never wavered in her support of me. She handed me a card with a name and phone number on it. I was told me to call this guy the next day after 2pm and set it up.

I learned my first lesson about networking that day. I called that number and received an appointment to interview. I accepted the job and moved on; hello networking, goodbye Ron!

I continued to use my networking abilities over the next 5-6 years. I made more money at each location than I did at the previous employer. I worked hard at improving my skill set and learning all I could about each job. I flat out worked harder than the people around me. This is how I moved up in the world without any college education. I moved to Florida in 2006.

It all came crashing down on me in January of 2009. My relationship with my first wife was broken. We both tried to repair it but we just couldn't find a way to make things work. I decided to leave. Then, as if I needed a little push, I was laid off at my job the next week. I was working a sales job attached to the housing market at the time. NOBODY was buying houses in Florida during 2008-2009, thus no one was spending money on anything connected to housing.

Additionally, we were upside down on our own house by more than $100,000. There was no way to make it work with the bank. I had to let it go as well. Yes, you read that correctly. I lost my house, job, and marriage in a three week span. I hit rock bottom. I had absolutely nothing going on for me right then in life. Everything I though we had built together was now gone.

I moved back to West Virginia in January of 2009. I needed emotional support and I didn't have anyone in Florida that I was especially close to. There were a lot of one way conversations with God in the next several months. I don't know if I won the battle, but I definitely screamed louder than he did. It took several months to get my head back on straight. I made a decision one night after another screaming fight with God. I needed to change my outlook on life. I had to rebuild from the bottom up. I needed a job to start my way back.

The funny thing is, I never chose the mattress industry. It chose me. In fact, I am pretty sure the sales recruiter thought I was an idiot, or deaf, or both. I answered on the third ring.

"Is this Donnie Masters?"

"Yes it is."

"This is Colleen from the Sleepy's recruiting team, how are you doing today?"

"Who?"

"This is Colleen from the Sleepy's recruiting team, how are you doing today?"

"WHO?!?"

"This is Colleen from the Sleepy's recruiting team, how are you doing today?"

"I'm sorry, but I have no idea why you're calling me. Did I apply to work for you?"

"No sir, you didn't. That is why I'm calling you."

Colleen and I talked for 15-20 minutes. She had found my resume online via Monster or CareerBuilder and was reaching out to see if I was still in need of employment. She said I had a set of skills that they were looking for. I entertained her flattering conversation and agreed to go to an interview with a Regional Manager the next day.

I was thoroughly impressed with the interview process and the man that interviewed me. Colleen had forwarded a copy of my resume to the Regional Manager I met with. He knew plenty about me before I even got there. We spoke for almost an hour about the position, the ability to be promoted, and the pay structure.

I agreed to take the position with Sleepy's as I was in dire need of employment. It was clearly the best opportunity I had been presented with during my almost year of unemployment. What I didn't know was that this decision was going to change my life forever.

Mix in some college education on and off over the years and there you have my story. I am not "wealthy" if we are measuring in strictly financial terms, but my life is so much better balanced than where I was in 2009. I get to write books. I have my own small business. I am inspiring others to win at life! I have learned so many things over the last 8 years that I can't wait to share with you.

CHAPTER 2
GOOD DEBT VS. BAD DEBT

I am going to anger some people right now by saying this in the very first paragraph of the chapter. Debt used properly can be a very positive momentum changing investment vehicle. In fact, debt used properly will change your life forever in a very positive way.

There is a legion of fans right now (the Dave Ramsey fanatics are lined up and picketing on my front lawn as you read this) that are screaming at the top of their lungs, "All debt is bad!" And in **most** cases I actually agree with them. However, if your goal is to grow your business and personal bank accounts to unbelievable levels of wealth, then there is going to come a day that you need to utilize debt in order to achieve your end result. I will repeat myself one more time so that we begin this chapter on the right foot. Used properly, debt is a blessing and an opportunity to outsize your gains on an investment.

So what is debt? According to Merriam-Webster, debt is defined as, "a state of being under obligation to pay or repay someone or something in return for something received". Any person, business, or government can borrow money and go into debt. In fact, debt is used by many corporations, governments, and individuals as a way of making large purchases that they do not have the cash on hand to purchase outright.

Once money has exchanged hands, a debt arrangement is then created. This "arrangement" offers the borrowing party permission to borrow a specific sum of money with certain financial terms and an agreement to pay it back at a later date in full, or over time, with interest of course.

Let's not get ahead of ourselves though. In order to clarify what using debt properly looks like, we must be able to distinguish between debt. Only once we can identify good and bad debt can we begin to make smarter financial decisions. So how do we distinguish between good debt and bad debt then?

Good Debt vs. Bad Debt

Since we have already defined debt as an amount of money borrowed by one party from another party, it is important to clarify that a party could be an individual, business, or government. Most people think of debt only as an individual person borrowing from a company. This is the most common type of debt in the United States.

Good debt should only be defined as an investment of capital that will generate additional income for you. Taking out student loans, for example, has been sold to consumers as a form of good debt. I disagree completely. The theory behind this college finance plan is that after your education is received from a higher education institute, your market value in the work force is higher than it was prior to having no education. This course of action is also supposed to create opportunities in your life to earn a larger income than others. I actually believe that this specifically taught theory was true at some point in time, but it is no longer relevant in today's new economy. There will be a lot more on this later.

Borrowing cash to buy a single family home has also been taught to consumers as a good debt. This is referred to as a mortgage. We are going to spend a lot of time breaking down mortgages in chapter 8, when we discuss real estate and business loans. Before we do though, let's be really clear about something up front. Buying a single family house to simply live in is not a good debt. Why you ask? Because it does not create income for you. It costs money out of your pocket every month to live in that house, even after all the supposed "tax breaks".

The only good thing about carrying a mortgage is that in ideal conditions your home WILL increase in value over time. In the right conditions, or rather the right housing market, these capital gains can be substantial and life changing. Unfortunately, the housing bubble here in the United States taught us that this is not always the case. Many people lost large sums of money during that crash by buying an "asset" to live in.

Bad debts, consist of money that is used to purchase items that depreciate in value over time. These items do not generate income for you, rather they actually cost you money to maintain or own them. The most popular examples of bad debt for individuals include cars, boats, RV's, and credit cards. For businesses, bad debt is taken on to finance any activity that does not generate additional profits.

This bad debt thing should sound pretty familiar to you. As real people that function on emotions rather than logic sometimes, we have all made mistakes in our lives. We have all done stupid with a lot of zeroes attached! No one here is judging you or your past actions. Just keep in mind as we go along in the book; it is your time to begin making better financial choices. Let's spend some of our energy on winning this game of money. Remember, you will be able to overcome any financial difficulties that you are facing now. We will also make sure that we are prepared for the "uh-oh's" of the future as well.

Why Can't I Just Be Debt Free?

There is a dedicated legion of fans that simply can not be ignored right now. They say you and I should live debt free forever. I think this theory sounds like a better plan than having too much bad debt of course, but it comes up short on the bigger picture. I personally believe that Dave Ramsey has good intentions, but I feel that his books and financial education does not take the average person far enough along the road of money. It is very easy to offer a general rule about being debt-free and here are the steps to do it.

Life is never simple and uncomplicated, however. Sometimes bad things happen to good people. Good things happen to bad people too. We are not all robots that can make decisions without emotions and feeling. If we could, then no one would be in over their heads. A simple chant about being debt free doesn't work for everybody.

Oddly enough I am not hating on Dave Ramsey or what he teaches. For a lot of people he offers hope and a chance to see the light at the end of the tunnel. I am simply pointing out that living your life by a general rule of never having debt may not be the best scenario for everyone on earth. I am a small business owner. I work full time for another small business. Neither of the businesses I am involved in have any debt on the books currently. That is in part to Dave Ramsey setting me straight about debt years ago.

My larger problem is that Dave Ramsey does not teach people to take calculated risks in order to exponentially raise their financial situation in life. Sometimes a business can grow overnight and with some extra cash at it's disposal, the business will generate much larger returns and profits. Sometimes in life, we will have opportunities to purchase items below value due to the overall market or an unique situation. Not even considering taking on debt will keep your eyes and wallet closed to some amazing opportunities that can come your way.

I have personally seen way too many people pass up an amazing opportunity just because they feared debt. They did not even want to consider increasing the amount of money coming into their household. This is just crazy! If I offered you $900 for $600 every month, you would take it, right? So why can we not have a mature and open conversation about financing a piece of rental real estate that offers that exact payout scenario? All because of some general rule about debt? I don't think so. With just a little bit of education, I believe it is much easier to understand the difference between good and bad debt as opposed to missing out on amazing opportunities in your life.

One more thing I would like to quickly add about debt in general. I personally love to categorize something as a good debt when someone else pays the debt for you. Take a multi-unit property as an example. If the tenants pay you rent in excess of the mortgage and related expenses and you get to live on site for free, what is the risk of that as opposed to owning a single family home?

To be sure, taking on debt is risky, and I am not saying it doesn't have legitimate concerns. What I am saying loud and clear is that sometimes the rewards can be extremely lucrative and life changing. With the help of this book, you will know when and how to evaluate such risks with clarity.

Good Debt

- Investment Real Estate

- Business Loans That Generate <u>Additional Profit</u>

Bad Debt

- Credit cards, consumer loans, and vehicle loans

- Business loans to cover expenses, equipment, payroll, or an increase in revenue without additional profits

One of the biggest problems facing our country today is that bad debts are just as risky as the good ones, but somehow in our American culture we have been sold on some of these demons as okay to live with. Specifically, there are four major lies that almost all Americans have been taught to believe as truth (don't worry, we cover them all in detail in the next chapter). These are all commonly accepted as debts that everyone is supposed to have as a passage into adulthood.

Furthermore, people should also know that some bad debt is better to have than other bad debt. For example, debt used to buy a personal residence is **MUCH** better than debt used to buy a car. At least when you buy a house there is an opportunity to profit when it is sold. That situation will never happen when buying a car or using a credit card. Ideally, you should look at bad debt the same way a business would. In terms of business accounting, bad debt is debt than can no longer be collected from a party. It is then considered an expense to the company. This is how you should look at ALL bad debt. It is an expense to your personal finances.

Having defined debt, and classified both good and bad debt, it is time to discuss managing your debt. Managing debt can be difficult and sometimes people do not have the financial means to pay off their bills. This can be due to a job loss, or reduction in income by having to switch jobs unexpectedly. Other times people simply get overwhelmed by their financial obligations and cannot decide on their best course of action.

If you find yourself in over your head as it pertains to credit cards. Seek out help. There are many options available for debt relief, and seeking the help of a company that provides debt counseling is usually the best course of action to take. A lot of individuals, myself included, have benefited from credit counseling services over the years. They can help you consolidate your debts and finished paying them off in a much shorter time frame.

In my early 20's I was one of these people that needed that kind of help. I understand where you are coming from if you also are struggling with credit card debt.

What works for most people, as it pertains to credit counseling, is that they get a few reasonable steps on how to become debt free from these credit counseling agencies. They help people in reaching settlement agreements with their debtors and make it possible for borrowers to consolidate their payments into one smaller payment each month.

Where these companies fail a majority of people is not educating them on getting out of <u>AND staying out of debt</u>. They do not educate people about their money behaviors or spending issues that got them in trouble to start with. They don't help prepare a budget or fix credit scores either. We continue to get short changed on our financial education.

So now the next big questions to answer are, who borrows money and why? Why is there a consistent record of getting into trouble with borrowed funds? All three are great questions that we will now discuss.

Types of Borrowers

So now that we have identified what debt is, the 2 types of debt, and why debt management is only a quick fix solution, it is time to talk about the reasons for borrowing money and who actually borrows it.

First, let's take a few minutes to talk about the different types of debt that individuals, businesses, and governments carry. Only after you can identify what debts you have AND why you borrowed money in the first place, can you start taking positive step towards becoming bad debt free.

Individuals

Examples of bad debts owned by individuals include mortgages, credit cards, and car loans. For most people, debt is a means of spending future income or earnings before it is actually earned. Frequently, people in industrialized nations use consumer loans to buy houses, cars, and other items considered too expensive to buy outright with cash.

Besides these more formal and legal debts, private individuals also lend money to other people; usually their relatives or friends. The reason for these "informal" debts is often because those who lack income or appropriate credit scores may not have access to affordable lines of credit. These type of debts can be a major cause of family issues, specifically when they are not paid back as agreed or in a timely manner.

Businesses

Corporations can have loans and credit card debt just like a consumer. In addition, corporations that need funds have other debt choices at their disposal. Bonds are not very common for small businesses, but larger companies use them frequently.

A company, just like an individual, can use multiple types of debt to finance its activities. Many small business have limited funds to start off with. The extra cash that these debts provide can come in handy during a financial emergency or when the company needs additional funds to close a profitable deal.

A **term loan** is the most common form of company debt. A term loan is a fairly simple agreement to lend a fixed amount of money for a fixed period of time. This amount is to be repaid by a certain date in the future, hence the "term". A term can be defined as any period of time, though it is usually measured in years. In most cases, interest is paid on these loans, either in one lump sum or in periodically agreed intervals; usually monthly.

A **syndicate loan** is a loan given to a company that wants to borrow more money than a single lender is willing to assume the risk on. This kind of loan is provided by an entire group of lenders and is arranged by several commercial banks with one bank taking a "lead" position in the deal.

As previously hinted at, a company can also issue **bonds**. Bonds are debt securities. They have a fixed period of time and a fixed payment schedule. Long term bonds are much less common than shorter ones.

A **letter of credit** can also be used to pay for a transaction. In most cases, a bank will issue a professional statement on corporate letterhead stating that you have "x" amount of credit with them. These are used mostly during international trade business agreements of a high dollar value. A letter of credit is also used frequently when suppliers and customers live in different countries where company credit scores and repayment information may be harder to get.

Governments

The government primarily issues bonds as debt to pay for major capital projects. These debts can be issued by local, state, or national governments. The rate of indebtedness by a government is calculated as a ratio of debt-to-GDP, or Gross Domestic Product. Governments use taxes as a source of income to make these payments at a later date.

So now that we know about the 3 different types of borrowers: individuals, businesses, and government; we must look at why debt has become a major issue in America. Specifically, why do we borrow money?

According to bankrate.com, the top 10 reasons why people have debt is a wide and varied list. I believe it is worth taking the time to dig into this subject in a little greater detail right away. Specifically, what happens to most individuals that they have chosen to incur debt as part of their everyday life choices?

Top 10 Reasons Individuals Have Debt

1. Reduction in Income/Same Expenses

2. Divorce

3. Poor Money Management

4. Underemployment

5. Gambling

6. Medical Expenses

7. Lack of Savings

8. No Money Communication Skills

9. Banking on a Windfall

10. Financial Illiteracy

What happens if you lose your job and have to get another one?Do you keep spending money the same way as you did before? In order to avoid going deep into debt, or even bankrupt, it is necessary to align your spending with your income. We will dedicate a section of this book to budgeting a little later on, but for now it is important to understand that leaving your spending patterns the same as before and mixing in a reduction of income, will put you in debt quickly.

People are also more likely to spend additional money when they use credit cards rather than when they spend cash in hand. This is because emotionally you are much farther away from the cash and are less likely to remember how much you have actually spent on that card by the time the bill comes. When the bill does finally arrive, most people have spent more money than they normally would have spent otherwise, increasing the debt load as you carry some of the balance into the next month. You must remember that credit card companies are counting on this to make a larger profit off of you.

Divorce appears on this list, which is quite enlightening. I will say one major thing about marriages. Marrying the wrong person will have a catastrophic effect on your finances long term. Many people have had to declare bankruptcy after a divorce. Bankruptcy means at least 3-5 years re-building your credit.

It is very important that you think long and hard about the person that you are considering having a long term relationship with. It might literally cost you an opportunity at a better life.

To some people this may sound harsh. But the reality is, that a well planned marriage will actually help both individuals obtain far more in life than they could by themselves. Think about the opportunity of working a small business together, saving for retirement together, and working towards your financial future as a team. If you can't do this with your current partner than it might just be time to reconsider your choice.

Next on the list of why individuals have debt is poor money management. I think we have spent enough time already talking about debt at this point and poor money decisions. We have a lot more to talk about in regards to money management as we progress in the book.

I will talk about poor money management in the next chapter, but I want you to remember that it's not your fault. Your financial education, or lack thereof, began with the public school system and ends with poor money decisions because of their teachings. There is a lot of concrete evidence for why this is not all your fault.

Underemployment is one of the biggest challenges facing America today. It has been said that as much as 25% of the workforce is working a job that is below their skill level. We are going to talk about this subject in detail later on when we tackle the subject of opening a business and why it matters to your long term wealth plan.

Number five on this list is gambling. Plain and simple, just don't do it! Believe me when I tell you I understand the thrill of gambling. It seems like with just a little luck and incredible timing, all your financial worries will go away. I can promise you that over the long term the only winner will be the casino or lottery.

Medical expenses are a major issue in America right now. We are going to discuss this in length when we talk about an emergency fund and why it is so important to have one for just this scenario. The seventh item on this list, lack of savings, also goes hand-in-hand with this subject.

In the first chapter, we talked a little bit about why Americans do not have any money communication skills. You were probably never taught any during all your "education". Hopefully, by the end of this book, that will no longer be the case.

As for the ninth item on this list, banking on a windfall, I don't even know where to begin. I wouldn't even know what to say when somebody tells me that their financial decisions are based on money coming to them at a much later date and time. Maybe I just have never been so lucky as to have someone who earned a ton of money wanting to just hand it over to me.

At this point, I would like to talk a little bit about the tenth item on this list, or financial illiteracy. I have already disclosed that I believe the public education system has failed the majority of Americans. I would now like to talk a little bit about how the rich get richer under a system of capitalism.

The main difference between the rich and the poor in America has everything to do with financial mindset. People that already have money, or those that create vast amounts of it, surround themselves with the best individuals to help them manage their money. They are often given special access to the best investment opportunities, the best real estate deals, and they can afford the best financial advice that money can buy.

The average person in America will receive no such advice. If you come from a situation where there was no money, then you most likely will receive no education about money. It is then up to you to educate yourself and make better financial decisions than the previous generation did.

What do the rich know about finance that the poor don't? Making a lot of money has nothing to do with wealth. It is how you spend the money that you have that determines wealth over the long term.

Just this past week, I was having a conversation with a very successful business owner. He makes hundreds of thousands of dollars each year, but he has many more liabilities than assets. The reason seems to be that while he has done incredible things in order to make his business successful, he has not devoted the time to learn how to properly manage his own money.

This is not a form of criticism to this specific person. As your income goes up, it is only natural to spend more money. It is usually what we are taught to do. No one is prepared to handle large amounts of money properly when they come out of the public education system.

We have been taught hard work will pay off. We have been taught to save for retirement and to turn our finances over to someone that is educated in money management. Think about your retirement accounts and how they are managed. The company that handles your retirement may or may not even know what your financial situation is.

The specific business owner that I was talking to had also taken someone's poor advice regarding his taxes. He now has to work even harder this year to pay his back taxes. A proper financial education may have prevented this situation. Just like our finances, we are often taught that taxes are "too difficult", so we need to hand them over to an accountant or CPA.

When do we say enough is enough? Can we ever draw a line a declare ourselves competent enough to handle our own money?

You need to learn enough about finances in order to seek assistance when it is needed. The answer to most problems with money, no matter your level of income, is knowledge. It takes knowledge to be financially free. We are focused on the wrong problem. Instead of worrying about increasing your income level, we should all be focusing on increasing our financial acumen. This will help everyone achieve at least some form of wealth.

If you ask a millionaire how they made so much money in life, they will tell you that one of their essential secrets was possessing a cross section of knowledge in business and finance. In other words, they never stop reading and learning about money!

In other words, your income level has nothing to do with your financial success or failure in life. How you spend your money that you receive does. Financial education will help you make smarter investment decisions and stop wasting money on junk.

So now that we have discovered that your current income level has nothing to do with your overall wealth, let's talk about a few ways to better manage the income you have coming in.

Tips for Managing Income

Most people work hard and earn a respectable income, yet they find it difficult to manage their finances. As a matter of fact, a lot of people spend their paycheck as soon as they get it. This is called being broke! Most of these same people will then live on credit cards until the next paycheck. That cycle of broken behavior has to be stopped if you want to win with money.

Many people are neck deep in debt and will never find their way out of the problem. They will declare bankruptcy and make the same mistakes again and again as they go through life. This is a major issue facing our nation today, as too many of our citizens are truly clueless about handling their money. Not only is it dangerous for one's personal well-being, but this kind of financial behavior can have a devastating effect on their relationships and their family units as well.

This problem of spending money too quickly can have a dangerous effect on worker productivity as well. People become demoralized and demotivated since they believe their take home pay is never enough money for the work they do. They then begin to feel alienated from other co-workers and do not perform their best anymore. Below are some great tips on how to manage your income and be a better, more productive employee.

1. Tell yourself that no matter how much you are earning, you will tailor your standard of living accordingly. You must adjust your mental process and make yourself believe that no amount of money is too big or too small to handle. You must live within your financial means every paycheck.

2. Do not elevate your expenses and lifestyle when you receive a pay raise. Create a good habit of saving the extra income for future use and opportunities.

3. Be wary of aggressive advertising. You should look at advertising as a means of separating your money from your wallet. Think about how long you have been able to live without that particular item you want to purchase so bad. Advertisements are created by manufacturers and retailers as a means to make more money from your emotions.

4. Do not buy on impulse, ever. Be disciplined enough to buy only those things you need and not the things you want. Wants are to be treated completely different from needs. Make a list of the items needed and purchase only that. Do not make any major financial decisions without sleeping on it first and involving your partner.

5. Reduce and eliminate your reliance on credit cards. Do not take your credit cards everywhere you go. Leave them at home if you have a spending problem so that you have to think about a purchase prior to buying it and leaving the store. Most people hate returning items. Retailers know this.

6. Maintain a level of discipline in regards to handling your money and maintaining your budget. Recognize small mistakes you make and adjust your budget for the future. Allow for small splurges and indulgences as rewards for doing well.

There is one more point that I really want to stress at this time. It is up to you, and only you, to choose to live a better financial life. Unfortunately, you may have to work harder than someone else to achieve this goal. You will make mistakes, and that's okay. No one is perfect and life is not fair. Deal with it, learn from it, and move on. You can gain control of your finances and your future. You can do it!

CHAPTER 3
YOU HAVE BEEN LIED TO

Have I previously mentioned my distaste for the public school system in America yet?. One of my biggest concerns with our nation today is that children are being taught years and years of English, Math, and Science. But in most cases, our kids graduate high school without having had one class in financial management.

Over the course of your working life, you will be expected to pay taxes, fund your retirement, and take care of yourself financially. I am not sure how we can expect our children to do this when they are not being taught how to do so. Additionally, the cards are stacked against most children as no one in the family has enough wealth to manage. This simply means that there is zero education at home as well.

Since at least the 1950's, and maybe longer, the American consumer has been fed four downright lies that have been ingrained in our culture as truth, even though logic and simple math tells us that it doesn't make sense. These four "truths" are that you must buy a house, you must get a college education, you must save a lot of money for retirement, and you must avoid all debt.

We are going to tackle all of these "truths" head on in this chapter, but we need to break them down one by one in order to make some sense out of it all. Let's start off with the grand daddy of them all. You must buy a house!

Big Lie #1 – You Must Buy a House

Most people can not just go out and buy a house with cash. They do not have that kind of money in their bank account ready to spend on a residence. In order to purchase a house then, most people must take out a mortgage to pay for their home. Since most people have to utilize a mortgage as part of the payment process, shouldn't we start by defining what a mortgage is?

Dictionary.com defines a mortgage as:

1. a conveyance of an interest in property as security for the repayment of money borrowed.

2. the deed by which such a transaction is effected.

3. the rights conferred by it, or the state of the property conveyed.

In plain language, a mortgage is a legal agreement that carries the conditional right of ownership of an asset by the owner to a lender as security for taking out a loan. In terms of real estate, the house acts as collateral for the lender. The lender's interests are then recorded in the register of the title documents to make it public information that they have an interest in a specific property. The mortgage agreement is then voided when the loan is fully repaid by the borrower.

I believe that there are three primary reasons people are told to purchase a home. If you take this advice at face value, it appears to be solid financial advice for a lot of practical reasons. But let's take a brief moment and really break down these three reasons that people buy a property to live in.

- **A home is an appreciating asset**

- **You get to lock in your payments**

- **I can sell it later on for a profit, or live in it "free" at retirement**

Let's start by talking about whether your personal home is an appreciating asset. Do you live in a single family home, townhouse, or condo? How much is your house going up in value every year?

USA Today conducted an interview with renown Yale economist and Nobel prize winner Robert Shiller. His direct quote is as follows:

"If you look at the history of the housing market, it hasn't been a good provider of capital gains. It is a provider of housing services...

Capital gains have not even been positive. From 1890 to 1990, real inflation-corrected home prices were virtually unchanged."

In other words, yes the house you live in will go up in value over time, but that value is merely keeping up with overall inflation. Your house is therefore **NOT** an appreciating asset. Furthermore, it does not produce income for you either, so we can't even classify it as a good debt.

Now someone is thinking okay, but you get to lock in your payments for the life of the loan, right? In theory yes you do. But do you know that your payments are still going to fluctuate every year anyway? Taxes on personal property can be outrageous depending on classification of the property and home values in the area. Every year taxes and insurance cost more than the year before. So yes, your payment on the mortgage and interest will stay the same, assuming that you locked in your mortgage rate, but your escrow will constantly adjust with the changing taxes and insurance rates. This means your payments will fluctuate over time.

All right! I hear someone else saying. Enough of this craziness! At least I get to live in my house "free" at retirement or I can sell it for a big capital gain later on in my life. Sure, if you say so. But before you believe that hype, answer me a question. How do you live in a house for free? Yes, maybe after 30 years you have paid off the mortgage, but taxes, insurance and utilities will be higher than they have ever been. Not only that, but how many upgrades and repairs have you had to do over 30 years? The true cost of home ownership is very high and it is most certainly not free.

Someone else is going, "hold on a minute here." I sold my house and got a big fat check with capital gains at closing. What can you say about that fella?

I could tell you that you would have done much better investing your money in the stock market over the same 30 years that you paid off your mortgage. Don't believe me about that one either?

According to the Washington Post:

"The Washington Post analyzed Shiller's data and reported that, over the past 100 years, home prices have only grown at a compound annual rate of 0.3%, adjusted for inflation. The S&P 500, on the other hand, has had an annual return of 6.5%. That's an awfully big difference."

I can certainly understand why many readers may need to re-attach their jaws right now. After all, I currently own a single family home, and I bet a lot of you do to. But what else am I going to do, sell my house and rent forever? No, and neither are you.

As with any legend or myth, there is some truth to this argument. The reality is, that being able to lock in your payment on an appreciating asset is a beautiful thing for your overall wealth accumulation. The problem is, that a single-family house is not an appreciating asset. So what is the best solution?

If you are going to buy a home to live in, I would suggest that you look into a 2-4 unit "multifamily" house. The reason why is incredibly simple to understand. Your private residence will now cost considerably less for you to live there, as other people will rent from you and help pay off the house. With some of these savings you can invest for your retirement sooner in life. Plus, you will build equity over time on a "good debt". We don't even need the house to appreciate in value to make this plan work. Let me explain this even farther.

A good debt produces income for you, right?. We have learned that part already in this book. If 3 out of your 4 units are paying rent to you then the property will produce income. This now makes your personal residence a good debt. The rent payments should cover all the mortgage due plus the taxes and insurance on the property. Having 3 paying units will allow you to live in your personal residence for next to nothing. You may even find a deal that allows you to live payment free on your personal residence. No monthly mortgage payments to live in your house, now that's how to start winning with money!

On top of all that, you are borrowing money in a property that will go up in value over time, even if it only keeps up with inflation. The best part is, the house can actually not appreciate in value and this will still be a winning formula. Maybe your personal residence's return on investment doesn't beat the stock market's return over time, but you have to live somewhere while you are alive. Why not let it be a property that works with you to achieve financial freedom long term.

So if you are going to take on all the risk of a mortgage (and a big one at that), wouldn't it at least make sense to understand what it all entails?

What's The Deal with Mortgages?

A mortgage is the most readily available home loan opportunity and what most people are familiar with. When it is truly a home mortgage however, only two different parties are involved; the homeowner and the bank. A loan is provided to the individual from the bank, with the home used as collateral for the length of the loan.

If the agreed payments aren't made on time, the bank can then begin the foreclosure process. They use the mortgage agreement to take over full control of the house. The bank will then sell the house in an attempt to recover the loan that had initially been given to the individual. Foreclosure homes are often sold via auction, as the bank wants to get back their funds as quickly as possible. The auction process will make the house being sold sell at a steep discount to the general market. This is because all auctions are sold "as-is", "where-is". In other words, you are buying the property in the shape you see it with all it's flaws.

The key factor in the foreclosure process is time. The process can be very time consuming for the bank involved. It often takes several months or up even up to a year to clear the legal system and finally gain possession of the house. Many states also have contingency plans where the homeowner can get the home back very late into the foreclosure process if they can catch up with their payments. Because of the time and money involved in the foreclosure process, most lenders prefer issuing a deed of trust instead.

Deed of Trust

In a deed of trust situation, a third party is involved. This third party is referred to as the "trustee", or he who holds ownership of the home until the loan is repaid in full. The homeowner is still responsible for making payments to the bank, and once they have repaid the loan, the trustee holding the deed of trust will release it to the individual.

The bank can reclaim the house if payments are not made, just as with a mortgage. The home is reclaimed directly from the trustee however, and the long, lengthy process of a mortgage is non existent. This is because both the bank and the individual never actually held title to the home. Banks prefer the deed of trust arrangement as they can get title to the property and resell it much faster than if a mortgage is in place. A deed of trust also reduces the administrative costs (read legal fees) and length of time between foreclosure and getting the home resold.

Ultimately, when it comes down to it, lenders will desire a deed of trust arrangement while buyers will want a mortgage. Not all states allow deeds of trust and the terms can differ dramatically from state to state. As such, if a bank is pushing for a deed of trust, you should review the state guidelines with a real estate attorney to ensure you clearly comprehend the risks and whether or not a mortgage is even available in your specific state.

Basic Components

As with all other types of installment loans, mortgages have interest and are scheduled to be repaid over a set period of time. Most mortgages are up to 30 years, though repayment plans up to 50 years can be had. All types of real property are secured with the property itself as collateral.

A mortgage is still the primary method used to finance private ownership of residential and commercial property in the United States. Although the methods will differ in various countries, the basic components are similar to ours. These are the common terms used in mortgages and deeds of trust.

Property: The physical residence being paid for. The exact form of ownership is determined by the agreement entered into; either a Deed of Trust or a Mortgage.

Mortgage/Deed of Trust: This is the secured interest of the lender in the property, which may or may not include restrictions on the use or disposal of the property.

Borrower: The person borrowing funds to finance the "asset" and is creating an ownership opportunity in the property.

Lender: The party offering the financing money, but it is usually a bank or financial institution.

Principal: The original total amount of the loan, this may sometimes include other costs. Whenever any principal is repaid, the principal amount will reduce in size.

Interest: The profit or financial reward gained by the lender for the use of their money over time.

Foreclosure or repossession: The process where the lender has to foreclose, repossess, or seize the property under certain situations.

Other terms are more prevalent in different countries, but the above referenced terms are the essential components of a mortgage in the United States. Most governments regulate areas of the banking and lending industries within their respective countries in order to prevent fraud.

Lenders provide loan funds for properties to earn interest income, or make profit. Lenders generally borrow these funds themselves since they do not have enough capital to lend over and over again without replenishing their coffers. The price at which other lenders lend out these monies affects the cost of borrowing as well. Lenders can also sell the mortgage loan to other parties after closing on the deal.

Mortgage lending also has to take into account the risk of default on the loan. In other words, the assumed risk is the likelihood that the funds lent will be repaid as agreed. If they are not repaid as agreed, the lender will foreclose on the real estate assets as we have previously mentioned. This is not the preferable method of most banks. Banks prefer to have the interest funds to re-invest for more interest. They are not interested in a property to maintain and sell.

Mortgage Underwriting

Once the mortgage application enters into the final stages of preparation, the loan application is moved to a mortgage underwriter. The underwriter verifies all the financial information that the applicant has provided, and makes sure it is correct and valid. Verification of the applicant's credit history will occur. The house is then appraised, or given a value relative to similar properties in the area.

The income and employment information of the applicant will also need to be confirmed by the underwriter. The underwriting process may take several days to complete. It is advisable to maintain your current employment and not open any new credit while undergoing the underwriting process. Any changes made to the applicant's credit score, employment records, and/or financial information can lead to the loan being denied.

In the case of a fixed rate mortgage, the interest rate remains fixed, or locked-in, for the duration of the loan. In the case of a monthly repayment plan, which most mortgages are, the payment will remain the same amount throughout the entire loan. Please note that the amount of escrow and taxes will fluctuate every year as we discussed earlier.

In an adjustable rate mortgage, the interest rate is generally fixed for a set period of time, after which it will periodically adjust up or down based on the market index. The rate may adjust monthly or annually under the terms of your financing agreement.

Adjustable rate mortgages are not to be taken lightly. Adjustable mortgages transfer the risk of rising interest rates from the lender to the borrower, and thus are largely used where fixed rate funding is difficult to obtain or prohibitively expensive. Since the risk is transferred to the borrower, the initial interest rate may be between, 0.5% and 2% lower than the average 30-year fixed rate. We do no recommend an adjustable rate mortgage for a primary residence.

The interest charged to a borrower will depend upon the credit risk and the interest rate risk. The mortgage origination and underwriting process involves checking several factors including, credit scores, debt relative to income, down payment available, and other current assets owned by the borrower. Jumbo mortgages (mortgages over $417,000 in most of the United States) and subprime lending (borrowers with a credit score under 620) are not supported by government guarantees and face much higher interest rates than standard mortgages.

Now that we have covered one of the biggest financial decisions you will make in your life, buying your personal residence, let's turn our attention to another big "truth" told in America today. You simply **MUST** get a college education.

Big Lie #2 – You Must Get a College Education

Okay, so maybe this was sound advice 50 years ago when a majority of people did not already have a college education, but it simply no longer applies in today's society. Most people can spend a fraction of college costs on certification and/or job training and find meaningful employment. Let's talk about student loan debt for a bit and why college is not a "good" debt.

In the United States, student loans were not even an option until the 1960's. In hindsight, a simple law that should have opened the door of opportunity to many more students, quickly got out of control. It took less than 20 years for reality to set in about student loans.

In 1958, the United States was only 13 years removed from World War II. Within our country, there was a legitimate concern about the spread of communism and how to combat it. Most people from the World War II generation will be able to recall the legitimate fear regarding communism. At one point, the United States even went as far as having public hearings, called the McCarthy hearings. Many high profile celebrities were called to testify before Congress in an attempt to expose communism among movie studios.

In an attempt to make sure that the United States stayed

competitive with the Soviet Union, especially in regards to math and science studies, Congress decided to pass the National Defense Education Act in 1958. In 1965, the Johnson administration created the guaranteed student loan, or Stafford loan program. Since 1965, the cost of a college education has outpaced inflation by more than 2 1/2 times.

According to an article entitled, "The History of Student Loans in Bankruptcy", the cost of a higher education amended for inflation is absolutely startling. According to the author of the referenced article, Steven M Palmer, in 1980, the average cost for tuition and room and board at a public institution was $7,587 adjusted for 2014 dollars. So what's the problem? By 2014 that same, exact education now cost $18,943; more than 2 ½ times the rate of inflation. Unfortunately, the news only gets worse as we go along.

If we continue down that same train of thought, loans are also becoming more necessary for someone who wishes to attend a college or university. In 1981, for example, someone who worked a minimum wage job could work full time in the summer and earn almost enough to cover their annual college costs. By 2005, that same student would have to work the entire year and use every penny of their earnings in order to attend school.

Between the years of 1958 and 1976, the United States government began to see a problem with their plan. Prior to 1976, student loans could be discharged in bankruptcy proceedings without any constraints whatsoever. As the economy began to sour in the 1970s however, change was enacted. The federal bankruptcy code was enacted in 1978, and the ability to get rid of student loan debt in bankruptcy was drastically changed.

The article goes on in detail, explaining that between 1978 and 1984, only private student loans could not be discharged in bankruptcy. As the situation continued to worsen, and more and more people were getting into debt via student loans, the government continued to restrict bankruptcy discharges.

Changes were made to bankruptcy laws in 1984, 1990, 1991, and 1992. In 1996 the federal government even allowed

Social Security benefits to be considered as income towards repaying defaulted student loans. In 1998 more changes were made again. By 2001, changes were made again allowing disability and retirement benefits to be considered as repayment income.

Basically, as the United States government became aware of the problem that they created, Congress continued to modify the bankruptcy laws, to make sure that student loans had to be paid back even when someone declared bankruptcy. They began changing the income requirements for repayment as well. Ask yourself a simple question, why is this?

Now that you have been informed of this new information about student loans, it should be obvious that student loans should always be considered a bad debt. In fact, let's continue to go into this a little deeper still. What about the fact that a college graduate will earn more money over their lifetime?

Technically, it is a true statement that a college graduate will earn more money over their lifetime of earnings than someone that does not attend college. But once again we are only being sold on part of the story. In reality, the average college graduate will not earn enough money to offset the student loan payments and interest accrued on their debt. In fact, a college degree isn't even a good indicator of whether or not you will get ahead in life.

Are Student Loans a Good Indicator of Success?

There can be no doubt that members of our government were simply trying to encourage its citizens to get a better education. This is most likely the reason that the laws were passed to help ensure every student could go to college if they wished to. So how did a good idea go so bad?

After World War II, the United States government saw the success of the G.I. Bill. The G.I. Bill ensured that military veterans would receive their college expenses paid for by the US government. Based upon the early success of the G.I. Bill, low interest loans were made available to all Americans by 1965.

The college graduation rate in the early 1960s was only 7 to 8% by the time most of these laws went into effect. In other words, a college graduate that was looking for a new job represented only one out of twelve applicants.

By today's standards, more than 30% of the population has at least a bachelors degree, and more than 60% has some college education, up to and including an Associates degree. At this point, the American workforce has so much education that almost everyone who applies for a job has some college education on their resume.

Based on the college graduation rate of the 1960s, the notion that higher education was better than entering the workforce straight out of high school became a common theme. Multiple generations of Americans have now been sold on this lie. At one point in time, statistics were presented that showed college graduates would earn as much as $3.4 million more in their lifetime than students who didn't graduate with a college education.

Unfortunately, due to the rising demand that student loans created, the cost of a college education began to rise much faster than the rate of overall inflation. This meant that families began to devote more of their income just to pay for college costs. At this point in time, annual tuition has entered into the tens of thousands of dollars per year. College expenses are so high that they have even outpaced families in the upper middle class. Many more students have had to turn to student loans to pay for their education, even if their family has some money set aside.

Today, more than 71% of students are leaving school with student loans, according to studentloanhero.com. Additionally, even though the average college graduate earns $17,500 more annually than a high school graduate, loans for a basic 4 year degree are now topping $60,000. A repayment on that type of loan equals a small mortgage payment in some parts of the United States. Students are dedicating $400-600 per month on student loan payments. According to the <u>Economist magazine</u>, this means that a lot of students with degrees are actually, "...worse off than if they had started working at 18."

With more and more students understanding that they are probably going to incur student loans as part of their education expenses, people have begun searching for ways to reduce college costs overall. Let's continue to go down this path of having a higher education at any cost.

The Dangers of Student Loan Debt

For high school students who are searching for ways to reduce the cost of a college education, your local community college has probably been pitched as a way to reduce your overall expenses and avoid larger debts by attending a more expensive four year university.

Many, if not all, financial advisers actually flat out recommend that you complete your first two years at a community college before transferring credits to a four year university. They claim that this is a sure fire way of cutting overall college costs by as much as half, thus minimizing your need for college loans. So far this sounds like really logical financial advice.

Community colleges usually have annual tuition rates that are well below those of a traditional four year college or university, and the two year route may really help in terms of overall cost management and the amount of student loan debt when finished. So where, exactly, is the problem with this plan?

As it turns out, statistically, community college students are more likely to struggle with their student loan debts **AND** are also more likely to default on payment of their student loans altogether. This doesn't seem to make any sense now does it?

According to pewtrusts.org, "38% of two-year college students who started to repay their loans in 2009 defaulted within five years..."

So the bigger question is, why do community colleges have this problem that doesn't seem to effect major universities?

The truth is that more people simply drop out of community college than a four year program. Some statistics report as many as 38% of community college students do not finish their program. Combine dropping out of school with the fact that high school graduates have lower paying jobs in the first place and you can clearly see the problem. A lot of community college students had to borrow money to live on while they went back to school which means they don't have extra money to repay the loans.

Even though tuition and overall costs are a lot lower at community college, the students are not as committed to finishing their degree there. Some of this can be explained by age and educational levels in the household (community colleges have older students and more immigrants), but much more of it involves lack of education about the cost of higher education.

Minimizing, and Managing Student Loan Debt

What do we make of all these default and delinquency rates for students trying to find a way into the working world? What do we say to high school graduates who are looking for ways to minimize the cost of a traditional college education by transferring credits from a community college?

The answer is to avoid student loan debt at all costs. It is a much better option to just work your way into better situations, promotions, and opportunities within the work force. The average person will actually do much better for not having the student loans wrapped around their neck for the rest of their life. Especially since student loans can not be discharged in bankruptcy.

If you aren't willing to take that as an acceptable answer,

please at least heed some sound financial advice on student loan debt. Below is a list of things to do or look for in order to avoid taking on more student loan debt than you will be able to handle later on.

- **Keep ALL other expenses as low as possible**

Managing or reducing your overall college expenses may mean living at home with your parents and packing your lunch instead of eating on campus every day. Working part time or full time while you go to school in order to pay for it is an even better idea.

- **Constantly be looking for scholarships and grants**

You can cut your college costs by seeking out scholarships and grants. Scholarships and grants provide you with financial aid that, unlike a student loan, does not need to be paid back.

If you're a working student, make friends with the human resources department at your employer. Some employers offer tuition reimbursement programs or professional development benefits that can help you reduce the cost of your education.

- **Always complete your degree program**

For college students who must rely on student loans to get through school, the single best predictor of successful repayment is actually graduation. Students who have completed their degree are the most likely to repay their school loans without defaulting.

"Just 15 percent of community college graduates default on their college loans, compared with 27 percent of community college dropouts," according to the Institute for Higher Education Policy.

Students who spend one year or less in school are the most likely to run into repayment problems on their student debt. This is often because they can't find a job or the job they do find doesn't pay enough to enable them to make their student loan payments on top of life's normal expenses.

- **Do not borrow more than is required**

Borrowing more than they need is very problematic for community college students because the federal education loan programs offer the same maximum loan amount regardless of what type of school you attend.

The maximum federal undergraduate loan available each year will typically cover the cost of all tuition and fees at a community college plus a few thousand dollars available for books, transportation, and living expenses.

That extra money can be very tempting to use. Living expenses pose a major challenge for many college students, regardless of what type of school you attend. How you plan to pay for your living expenses while in college can mean the difference between manageable and unmanageable levels of debt when you finish.

Having a plan to pay for your living expenses without resorting to maxing out your student loans will significantly reduce the amount of money you need in order to complete your degree. The less student loan debt you have when you graduate, the lower, and more manageable, your monthly payments will be. Having lower payments also means you will be able to pay those loans off faster.

Before we conclude this section on student loans, I believe it is important to cover the different types of student loans and how they can impact your financial future.

Not All Student Loans Are Created Equal

Federal education loans are issued directly by the federal government and they carry a fixed (locked in) interest rate, along with very flexible repayment terms. Federal student loans also have multiple options for postponing or reducing monthly payments based on financial circumstances. Federal student loans are generally low cost and lower interest loans.

Private education loans, which are not issued by the government, are issued by banks, credit unions, and other private lenders. These loans often have variable rates. Private loans are credit based loans that typically carry higher fees and interest rates than their federal counterparts. Private student loans offer fewer options for financially distressed borrowers to be able to postpone or reduce their payments as well.

One major difference between typical consumer loans (think auto loan) and a student loan is the deferment period. With a car loan, payments on the principal begin almost immediately, even if they are relatively small at first. In other words, with every payment made you are slowly paying down the total balance of the loan.

In contrast, all federal education loans and a lot of private education loans allow students to defer making any payments while the student is still in school. The repayment of the loan is then delayed for years in most cases while the student finishes their education. This comes with a cost of course, as there is not a delay on interest charges.

Except in the case of subsidized federal student loans (in which the government will cover the interest while a student is in school and are also awarded only to students who demonstrate the most financial need), interest begins to accumulate on college loans as soon as the loans are issued, even if a student is deferring payments.

This accumulation of interest may take place over months or years, quietly running up the balance on a student's school loan debt to alarmingly high levels.

If we add up all of these small details about student loans, then we begin to understand the much larger picture. Yes, it is true that college graduates will make more money than non-college graduates. The problem with that mathematical equation however, is that we are not calculating the amount of interest and debt repayments that come out of that extra income. When you begin to peel away the layers, we get a much clearer picture.

At this point in time, it just does not make any mathematical sense to enroll in college **UNLESS** you have a clear path to a high paying career. The amount of debt that one must take on in order to complete a basic four year degree far outweighs the difference in income for an average degree. If you are not looking at a masters or doctorate level career, then I believe the additional income to be truly insignificant for the amount of debt that you will have to incur.

The math no longer makes sense for kids to accumulate debt in order to get a basic degree now does it? That is why America is still being sold on something that no longer applies in today's new economy. Going to school after high school still helps you earn more money longer term. Unfortunately, the gap is closing quickly for a lot of majors. When you figure in years and years of loan payments that accumulate interest and never go away, the math becomes a lot clearer.

For further reading and research on this topic, I suggest this article. The article, by Nikelle Murphy, specifically points out 10 college degrees that are almost worthless to employers now. Not only is it a great read, but it may help you make a much better decision in life.

I think there is one more point that needs to be made at this time. The new economy that involves the Internet has also broken down the barriers between educated and non-educated citizens. Much like Bill Gates and Steve Jobs did to the computer industry years ago, so has the Internet done to this generation. You literally have college dropouts, high school dropouts, and teenagers, making vast sums of money via the Internet.

While it is important to note that this path is not for everyone, not attending college and pursuing your own business via the Internet is a viable option for some people. If your long term plan does not involve traditional education than you should heavily consider an Internet based business. I specifically like creative and art driven people to consider this road of success as opposed to "graphic design" schools.

Now let's tackle the next myth head on. That is, you must save a lot of money in order to retire.

Big Lie #3 – You Must Save A Lot Of Money For Retirement

How much money do you need to retire? One million? Two million? More or less than that amount?

No one, and I mean absolutely no one, has a realistic number that you can just plug in and use as a goal for your retirement accounts. The reason why is because one thing is constant in the world we live in, inflation.

Inflation is defined as:

"A sustained, rapid increase in prices, as measured by some broad index (such as Consumer Price Index) over months or years, and mirrored in the correspondingly decreasing purchasing power of the currency." This definition is according to businessdictionary.com.

So what does inflation have to do with America being sold a big lie about saving money for retirement?

The truth is you will never be able to save enough for retirement. Even if you were to put away 20% of your before tax income from the day you turned 21, you will never have enough for retirement without generating additional income. How can I be so sure this is true? Inflation erosion.

I can hear some of you rolling your eyes already. You are probably going back in time and imagining the job you had a 21, and starting to calculate what 20% of your before tax income would have been. I will save you the math.

Let's assume for the sake of argument that you earned $100,000 per year, every year for 40 years. In this example, you would have earned $4 million in your adult life. You were also one of the lucky ones, and you were able to retire at the age of 61 since you saved so diligently.

Now using these exact numbers, 20% of your pretax income

would be $800,000. But let's also assume that you invested wisely, and that you were able to grow your $800,000 retirement fund by a 250% return over the 40 years. $800,000 times 250% equals $2 million. A lot of you reading this right now are probably going that's incredible! I agree completely.

So what is inflation erosion and what does it have to do with my retirement account you ask? Inflation erosion is a technical term based on the belief that savings are being erased faster than ever because inflation is rising faster than the average income.

So at this point, you are probably asking how I can be so confident in my mathematical calculations? As it turns out, once again the United States government is supplying all the information we need. Specifically, the United States Bureau of Labor Statistics produced the following chart attempting to track inflation for just one 12 month period.

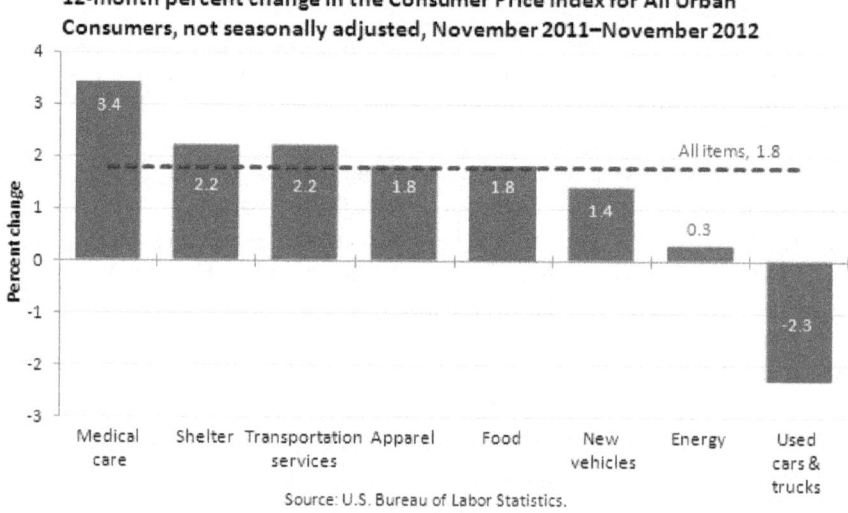

12-month percent change in the Consumer Price Index for All Urban Consumers, not seasonally adjusted, November 2011–November 2012

Source: U.S. Bureau of Labor Statistics.

The base line for inflation is 1.8% per year for the 2011-2012 period referenced in the above chart. In reality, medical care is almost doubling the rate of inflation every year. Additionally, housing and transportation services are outpacing inflation as well. If we add in discretionary spending, such as higher education and new cars you can see why your dollar is not going as far as it used to. There is no way to "out save" inflation.

So going back to our example, you retire at the age of 61 with $2 million in your retirement account. The problem is, based upon inflation, that $2 million doesn't go near as far as it used to. Let's look at a really specific example.

The exact same Bureau of Labor Statistics, has a really neat online calculator. This online calculator will show you exactly what inflation has done to the US dollar over time.

For our specific example, a person working for 40 years between the ages of 1960 and the year 2000 would retire with a $2 million retirement account. However, in order to have the same spending power in the year 2000 that their money had in the year 1960 when they started saving, you would have needed to accumulate $11,522,184.30.

Yes you just read that correctly, in order to have the same spending power that $2 million had in 1960, by the year 2000 and you would have needed more than $11 million! Unfortunately, I don't see any scenario in which this gets better going forward.

But there's another other thing I'd like to point out as well. During the years 1960 and the year 2000, a majority of working Americans received some form of pension and will collect full Social Security payments. I want to stress to you that I'm not making a political point here, but rather I am telling you that my generation and the generations behind me will not receive pensions. They simply do not exist anymore in today's world. As for Social Security, it's anybody's guess how long that's going to stay around.

To make this new information sound even more dire, this specific data was supplied by the US Bureau of Labor Statistics. Yes, the United States government acknowledges that this is a real mess and has zero solutions to fix it. Obama care? Trump care? Neither one will fix the mess that insurance providers, politicians, and pharmaceutical companies have created when it comes to healthcare.

Now let's talk about your income for just a moment. Are you currently making $100,000 per year? Are you even making more money than you did last year? Are you making more money than you ever have in your life? Probably not.

According to USA Today, Americans finally got a raise in income level during the 2015 tax year. The article says that incomes rose for the first time in 8 years, meaning that incomes had not risen at all since 2007. The same article continues on stating that most Americans don't feel like they got a raise in income because after adjusting for inflation their true level of income has not matched the levels of 1999. Depressing isn't it?

So for 16 years straight, the average US household has made less money than before. Once again the data was supplied by our own government. The data for this specific USA Today article was supplied by the United States Census Bureau. The same government that is supposed to be guiding it's citizens and providing a portion of their retirement has acknowledged that it is failing you.

Is Social Security even going to be available for another generation? Are we creating more jobs that pay a real living wage? Are expenses going down every year? Are incomes going up? The answer to all of those questions is "no", and I don't see any reason to believe they are going to be fixed any time soon.

So now we come to the fourth and final lie that is being taught to most Americans, you must avoid all debt in order to succeed in life. Debt is evil! All debt is bad! The credit card companies are ruthless with their aggressive advertising!

Do me a small favor and hear me out on this next part. It really might just change the way you look at things going forward in your life.

Big Lie #4 – You Must Avoid ALL Debt

Ah, yes. Stand up my Dave Ramsey loyalists and scream at

me! **ALL DEBT IS BAD!**

What if I could prove to you it isn't? In fact, what if I could show you documented proof that debt can actually make you wealthy beyond your wildest dreams?

You have probably heard some stupid expression over the years about how 90% of all millionaires got to millionaire status by investing in real estate. Think back to where you first heard such a crazy thing. Was it a friend that said it?

At one time in life, I repeated this to people as well. In fact, just last year I wrote a blog post that referenced the fact that 90% of millionaires started in real estate. I am guessing that this expression started somewhere in the real estate circle years ago. Most likely a Realtor or mortgage broker started this silly expression trying to convince someone to buy real estate. Can you become a millionaire by owning real estate? Yes. Did 90% of all millionaires achieve their wealth through real estate? No.

According to an article, on Financial Uproar, most millionaires do in fact OWN real estate, but a good portion of them did not use real estate to become wealthy. According to their own admission:

"...90% of millionaires do not come from real estate. Most millionaires come from a combination of success at work, owning a business, and investments, mostly in equities."

So why do we assume that people who have loads of debt in real estate holdings are wealthy? Does owning something other than your own house make sense long term? Absolutely, as long as it is purchased, repaired, maintained, and managed correctly.

The case for using real estate as part of your personal wealth building plan is a strong one as long as you follow all the rules outlined below. If you want to make money in real estate you must follow the path that many before you have laid out.

The 4 Rules of Investing in Real Estate

1. Cash Flow

2. Buy Below Market

3. Use Leverage Correctly

4. Take Every Tax Advantage

The cash flow on an investment in real estate must be positive by as much as possible. Simply put, the difference between what you can rent the property for and your mortgage payment must be a positive number. In order to not get into financial trouble down the line, you must be able to put this money away for future repairs and unexpected bills.

I do also want to make one more note here. There are a portion of real estate investors that believe buying the right property at any price is advisable. Based upon their beliefs, they will argue that depreciation, amortization, and the tax benefits of owning real estate as an investment, will make up for any cash flow losses. I strongly urge you not to listen to this advice.

As with any other investment, there are a multitude of general rules that are being taught on the Internet. My biggest suggestion would be to listen to someone that actually owns investment real estate as opposed to someone writing an article on it. If you simply ask for assistance, most people will be willing to share their opinions and advice about their own business.

Buying below market is paramount to making future gains on your property. Paying down the mortgage alone is not great use of your money. We have already looked at why that doesn't work very well. If you can not add value to a property between the time you buy and the time you sell, then you must get a discount when buying it.

We have already outlined good debt and bad debt. Using debt to make money is a good debt. If you can lock in a payment on the property that offers positive cash flow, then you are making money by using debt. Leverage should never be a long term plan by itself. Use debt along with the other 3 rules to make money.

I would also strongly advise against taking large loans against the property. While in some cases you may be able to get financing up to 95% of the purchase price, I would not advise going this route. The only time that it makes sense not to use a large down payment, is when you are planning to flip a property within a two year time frame. If you are truly buying an investment property, then you probably have no plans of selling it anytime soon, so lock in a great rate with no PMI (private mortgage insurance).

You must also take every single tax advantage available to you as well. Hire a good accountant or pay for professional advice if you are in doubt about anything. The tax advantages of owning rental real estate along with positive cash flow can be simply astounding over the long term.

There are two terms that you also need to become really familiar with. I have already hinted at it, but depreciation and amortization are your friends. I will quickly define both below.

Depreciation is defined as being able to write down the value of an asset over time, based upon common wear and tear.

Amortization on the other hand, is the ability to offset your income by deducting the loan payments as they are incurred. In other words, you will be able to deduct the interest expenses of the mortgage, and a portion of the principal, against the property's rental income.

I am going to really stress that ALL 4 of these things must be present in order to make it a good investment. If any of the 4 rules are missing in the deal, then you are taking on an extremely risky debt. Don't do it!

Are their other examples of using debt other than just real estate to help build wealth? Yes.

Many people have borrowed money to start a business, or take their business to the next level. Remember the rule of using debt, if you can make more money by using debt than it is worth considering.

I want to also stress one key point about business loans. Borrowing money to simply increase a business's revenue without being able to generate additional profits, is just plain stupid. In order to even consider taking on a business loan, you must be able to mathematically prove that the additional profits would be more than enough to repay the loan.

Let me say that one more time to make sure everyone hears this clearly. Before you even consider talking about a business loan, you must be able to mathematically prove that the additional profits generated would be more than enough to repay the loan. I prefer to use a calculation of 2-3 times more profit dollars for the risk of taking on a loan.

We have now clarified what the four "truths" are that Americans have been taught when it comes to personal finances. Additionally, I hope that I have also provided some factual evidence for why I believe that these four truths are not sound financial advice going forward.

So now that we know excelling at work, having a business, and making smart investments in both real estate and stocks are the key to your financial future, let's get right into starting your own business.

CHAPTER 4
START A BUSINESS NOW

I literally want you to stop reading this right now and get on your specific state's business website and look into forming a business. Please do it right this second!

Now that you have figured out where to file your application for a new business, let's talk business structure for a moment and why it matters. I need you to think really, really big for this part.

How big is your business going to grow over time? Do you know? Nope, me either. I don't have any idea whether I will have one new follower on Facebook, or sell 1,000,000 copies of this book and retire in the Bahamas. That is why it is critical to make sure your business is set up to take off **WHEN** you hit on your big idea. Please be sure to consider business formation seriously as it can have major tax implications later down the line.

First things first. What is a business?

A business is a living, breathing entity that acts as its own person. In the eyes of the government, your business is treated like a living human being.

There are several types of business entities ranging from a sole proprietorship to the multi-national "C" Corporation. It is very important that you look into what types of business formations are recognized within your state and local jurisdictions. Each of these "corporate entities" has it's own strengths and weaknesses which we will discuss here.

This next section contains the strength and weakness comparisons for each type of corporate structure commonly found in the United States. This part is meant to be a quick summation and not legal advice or guidance. If you are confused about anything or have questions that are not covered within the scope of this book, please seek out a tax attorney or accountant to help explain all of your options in detail. Remember that it is crucial to get this part correct before commencing business operations. A little money spent here on guidance and expertise can save you thousands of dollars down the line.

As a quick side note, the U.S. Small Business Administration has a section of their website that is very good at explaining in detail the different business structures here. I will summarize it for you below.

Types of Business Entities

Sole Proprietorship - This entity is very easy to set up. There is only one owner and there is no legal difference between the owner and the business. This is the simplest corporate entity. The owner does all the work, he/she gets all the credit, he/she takes all the profits, he/she absorbs all the losses. In the event of any legal liability, the owner is liable for all actions of the business.

On the set up side, a sole proprietorship comes with the least amount of paperwork, and you can use your business expenses as a tax deduction. One of the biggest negative aspects is that when you get into debt with the business and happen to default on said debt, the creditor can dig into your personal assets for recovery of any money due.

Advantages

- Owner gets all the profits/losses

- Easier to start up

- Low or no cost organization fees

- No legal documents are needed at start up

- The sole owner is free to make all decisions concerning business operations

- Owner pays income taxes on the profit made

Disadvantages

- Owner is solely responsible for all the liabilities taken on by the business. If the business does not have enough cash to pay back business debts, creditors can take the personal assets of the owner.

- An owner's ability to raise capital is limited to personal funds and the funds from people who are willing to give the owner loans.

- The business will close upon the owner's death; it does not continue unless transferred to the heirs of the estate. When it is transferred to the heirs, a new entity must be created.

Partnership - This is a legal entity which can have several people as owners bound in a legal working contract. The profits and losses are shared according to the terms stated in that contract, but they have unlimited liability for the business. In other words, their personal assets can be targeted in cases of default on debt or legal actions taken against them.

This type of entity usually involves larger amounts of start up capital than the sole proprietorship, as more than one owner is involved. A partnership does come with its own peculiar disadvantages as well. Partnerships can and do fail. People can be unpredictable when their hard earned money is at risk. I've seen more than one business partnership fall apart because of poor behavior, money issues, and relationships gone bad.

Advantages

- Business does not pay income tax, rather each owner claims their portion of profits/losses on their personal income taxes

- It is easy to start up and close

- Ability to raise funds among all partners involved

- A combined pool of knowledge, skills, and contacts

- Improved management of employees; Employees are managed by more than one owner

Disadvantages

- Partners are liable for every obligation of the business including contracts, torts, and any breaches of trust

- If any one partner has been sued and cannot pay the other party the full amount of the obligation, the third party may collect the money from any of the remaining partners involved

- Each partner is individually liable for the debts and obligations of the business; if the business does not have enough assets to pay back business debts, creditors can possess the personal assets of the partners

- A partner cannot transfer their interest in the business without the unanimous consent of every one of the other partners.

- Partnerships can become unstable due to the danger of one

partner wanting to withdraw from the business or dying.

The Different Types Of Corporations

C Corporation - is a separate legal and tax entity created by individuals who form the company. These individuals are called shareholders and offer money, property or both for the corporation's initial capital stock. The corporation is completely separate from those who manage the running of the business.

Advantages

- There is a pooling of capital from many investors and it is very easy to get the business up and running

- Shareholders are not responsible for the debts of the corporation

- If the corporation fails, shareholders will lose their investments in the corporation, but are not personally responsible for the corporation's debts

Disadvantages

- Double taxation; The profits of the corporation are taxed as they are earned at a corporate level, and dividends paid out by the company are also taxed on the shareholders personal income taxes

- Shareholders that control and own a large amount, or majority, of the corporation's voting stock have a dominant voice in the management of the business in comparison to shareholders that do not own as much stock

S Corporation - A business may "elect" to become an S Corporation (S Corp for short) in order to avoid income taxes at the corporate level, while at the same time retaining the advantage of limited liability that corporations enjoy.

Advantages

- Income is taxed only at the shareholder level, not at the corporate level, which means that an S Corp avoids the double taxation that C Corps have

- Shareholders are not held personally liable for the debts of the corporation

Disadvantages

- Shareholders that control and own a significant amount, or majority of the corporation's voting stock have a dominant voice compared to shareholders that do not own as much stock

Limited Liability Companies - A hybrid between a partnership and a corporation. Often called LLC's for short, they offer the limited liability of a corporation but the tax advantages of a partnership.

Advantages

- Profits pass through the LLC and taxes are paid personally by the members (owners) of the company

- Liability of the members is simply limited to the amount of their investments

- Members are allowed to participate completely in management of the company

- Other corporations and partnerships can be LLC members. There are no limits on the number of members for a LLC

- A LLC can have just one member

- Offers flexibility as it pertains to ownership; members decide how to operate daily business through the operating agreement

Disadvantages

- There is increased complexity in business formation; a LLC may be classified as a sole-proprietorship, a partnership, or a corporation for tax purposes

As you can see, each business entity has its own advantages and disadvantages. Why is this that important? One simple reason. How you structure your business will impact your ability to attract investors and grow the business long term.

When an investor is ready to open his/her checkbook to you, they want to see the viability of their investment based on the legal formation of the business. All business entities, whether they have limited or unlimited liability, are required to be registered with their state of formation. An investor wants to know how much of their portfolio is truly at risk.

Try to look at things from the other side of the coin for just a moment. If you were an investor, and you knew that investing in a certain business opens you up to a lot more financial liability, would you be comfortable investing a lot of money? Furthermore, would you even be comfortable investing at all?

Tax Breaks

There is an old saying that there are only three permanent things in life: change, death, and taxes. A country will never be able to survive and generate income if it does not tax its citizens. The problem with taxes is that they reduce your personal income. Large corporations pay millions of dollars in taxes every year. On a personal level, having that extra money means you could have spent it on other things such as growing your business, or maybe even a well deserved vacation.

But here's some really good news, when you start a small business you get to enjoy certain tax breaks for doing so. Tax deductions actually decrease how much money you give to the government at the end of the year. The one big caveat is that you must always properly account for all of your deductions on your taxes. Here are a few of my favorite deductions on a personal tax level.

Charitable Contributions

Generosity benefits you, literally. Out-of-pocket charitable contributions, no matter how small they are, can be deducted from your taxes every year. You will need some type of recognition from the charitable institution as proof. Usually a printed receipt of your donation will be enough evidence to take the deduction.

Student Loan Interest

To be asked to pay your student loan debts can be a burden on you financially. The good news is that a tax deduction is almost always possible. In most instances, you can actually deduct your interest payments up to $2,500 per year. This is of course provided that the debt was paid by you and NOT by your parents. Student loan repayments from parents are seen by the IRS as a gift to the child who is the one ultimately responsible for the loans.

Job Search Expenses:

If you are searching for a job, then you should keep tabs on how much you're spending while doing so. In other words, you should keep record of the amount of money spent while trying to find employment. Unfortunately, this deduction can be a little complex, so it is usually best to seek professional advice.

Energy Savings Credit

A tax credit is one of one the best reasons why you should go green, especially for your personal residence. You can deduct as much as 30 percent of your total home improvement costs depending on the improvements made.

A lot of people don't enjoy tax breaks for one simple reason, they don't know anything about the tax code and how to deduct legitimate expenses. Whether you are preparing your own taxes, or having them done by someone else, you need to be extremely organized with receipts and proof of deductions in the event of an audit.

Tax Breaks Available for Your Home Business

Owning a small, home based business can have huge tax advantages compared to working outside of your home. Here are some of the tax deductions available to home based businesses and how they work.

One of the best tax breaks is that you are now paying yourself instead of an employer paying you. This means you can control your paycheck, bonuses, and how much tax you have to pay to some extent. More money can go in your pocket as a result of a bigger paycheck or as profit for the business. You should work with your accountant or tax attorney to see which is more beneficial for your specific situation.

Your new company can pay for some things that come out of your personal pocket at your current job. For example, a business can provide retirement accounts to it's employees at no charge. The business writes off the costs of managing the plan, as well as the contributions to its employees. You can set up a fully funded retirement account without having personally contributed one single dollar out of your paycheck. Also, businesses can pay for all insurance needs of the employees. Again, the business writes it off as part of doing business. You get to select great insurance plans for your family.

There are some more major tax breaks when you own your own business at home. One of them is your car. If you take any trips in your car that have to do with your business, even if it is just driving to the bank to make a deposit, you can deduct the miles. Driving to the post office for stamps, going out to send a fax, and buying supplies are some more examples of what you can claim on your income tax as a deduction for your business. In fact, this can also be done if you are going down to buy groceries and buy some printing paper for your business during the same trip. Make sure you make the business trip first in order to be tax deductible.

Another example of business tax breaks is when you decide to take your family out for dinner. As you are sitting at the table, you notice that the waitress is really not enjoying her job, you then decide to strike up a conversation with her about working at home. At the end of the conversation you hand her your business card. You can now claim the trip to the restaurant as a business expense and you can claim the meal as an expense as well. Gotta love working for yourself!

This leads us to another tax break.

Vacations to any destination with your family can be also be claimed on your business taxes if you include some kind of business action during the trip. For instance, when you take your kids to a family friendly amusement park in Southern California (no I don't have a financial relationship with the D company), you can just happen to have a client that lives not too far from your end destination. You make arrangements to meet your client for dinner while you are in town, and during dinner you talk about business in some capacity. You can now claim the whole cost of flying or driving as a business trip on your taxes. A little warning however. The government does not think deducting your partner's and children's expenses is the least bit amusing, especially if they are not employed by the company.

Another big tax break, is your home office itself. The government has different rules on what you can claim, and what you can't claim, as a home office. You usually have to have a specific area in your home that can be enclosed away from the other areas of your house.

One of the things that a lot of business owners do not think about is claiming their business equipment on their income taxes as well. If you made a purchase of a desk top computer that will help you to build your business, then you can then claim that computer as a business expense. Also, the printing paper that you purchased for your business and even your web hosting can be claimed as an expense.

These are just a few examples of the many ways you can get big tax breaks for running your own business. There are literally hundreds of ways to save on taxes by owning a small business at home. A few pieces of advice I will give is to make sure you have an excellent accountant who is familiar with business taxes assist you, and please make sure you keep all receipts so that you have proof of your expenses should you ever get audited.

As I have previously stated, I currently work full time as an accountant for a small business, and I also have my own small business, The Masters Investment Group. I make all of these recommendations knowing that they are fully deductible as a cost of doing business. In order to better assist your record keeping, I have compiled and listed below some very common expense accounts for any and all small businesses. Please feel free to use this list as a general guide when setting up your company. Remember, if you are ever in doubt about the legitimacy of a deduction, please consult professional advice.

Common Business Expenses

Advertising and Promotion Expenses

Automobile Expenses

Bank Service Charges

Business Licenses and Permits

Computer and Internet Expenses

Continuing Education

Depreciation Expense

Dues and Subscriptions

Insurance Expense

Interest Expense

Meals and Entertainment

Office Supplies

Payroll Expenses

Postage and Delivery

Printing and Reproduction

Professional Fees

Rent Expense

Telephone Expenses

Travel Expenses

Utilities Expense

Ask My Accountant

I would like to specifically point out the last expense account that I listed, "Ask My Accountant". For anyone that is brand-new to business, or for any reason you are unsure of how to account for a specific expense, having this expense account will act as a catch all and remind you to ask about certain transactions when it comes tax time.

Another thing that is also worth mentioning here is that each of these accounts can also have sub-accounts. For example, the first expense category that I listed, "advertising and promotion expense", can have multiple sub-accounts in order to be more beneficial to your specific business.

In order to help me explain this in greater detail, I will share a little bit about my own company. For the purposes of my own small business, a category such as advertising and promotion expense is much too broad. I need to keep track of more specific data.

My small company needs to keep track of the amount of advertising and promotion dollars spent across multiple categories. Therefore, we have the broader general category, advertising and promotion expense, broken down into three very specific sub-accounts. Our three specific expense accounts are Amazon, Google, and book promotions. By breaking down our advertising and promotional expenses into three specific sub-accounts, we can quickly find out how much money we have spent on each specific advertising source.

In some cases, this much information is not necessary for your business. In my case, and for my business, I need to know which method of advertising is the most cost-effective for me. I would not be able to do that if everything was lumped into one broad, general category.

Owning a Business is the Key to Financial Freedom

So far during this chapter we have looked at business formation, personal tax breaks, business tax breaks, and some common expenses for all types of business. At this point, you might be asking yourself why is all this so important?

If you remember a little earlier on in the book, people that have accumulated substantial wealth cited four specific principles that helped them achieve their financial success. Those four specific principles were excelling at work, owning a small business, and investments in real estate and/or equities. This is why we are spending so much time on business related matters.

When beginning your own small business, one of the most common problems that people face will be funding. Besides having enough money to fund your dream, you also have to be able to promote and advertise your products and services to the people that are going to place down their hard earned money. Both of these things take sums of money.

Let's be really honest with each other for a moment, starting your own business is difficult. There is a very good reason why a majority of new businesses fail within five years of opening. But what if there was a way to start a business that guaranteed you funding and a proven business model?What if you could instantly have customers the moment that you opened your front doors?

For those people that have larger amounts of capital, I would recommend business franchising. One of the biggest advantages that franchising can offer is instant brand recognition and customers. This is because that particular brand is already recognized by a majority of people. You should not have any problem selling the products your franchise carries or produces. One quick caveat though, you need to make sure that you choose a well-known business franchise in order for you succeed.

For example, if your dream is to open a restaurant, it would be a much better idea to franchise a popular chain rather than to try and do it all on your own. This way, more people will know about the type of food you are selling and you will not need to advertise much, if at all in the beginning. Speaking of advertising, you shouldn't have to worry too much about it at all as the parent company usually does a lot of advertising for you. In most cases, the franchise company will also give you posters and other advertising products for promotions. If you are fortunate enough to join a large, national business franchise, you will enjoy the benefits of having television commercials for your business as well.

A business franchise will also provide you with employee and management training services. This way, you and your new employees will get hands on training prior to opening your business. This will be a huge help in both getting started, and smoothing things out in terms of finding and hiring quality employees. Health insurance availability and payroll support are also usually included in the training.

You have to work hard when you own a business franchise, and even that may not be enough to succeed. You also need to have a solid business plan, and a good location to start your business franchise. A good location should be accessible for your potential customers, as well as being brightly lit and well maintained. Computer systems, store policies, store layout, service standards, and even management practices need to be planned out way ahead of opening day.

When beginning a business franchise, you also have to know certain aspects of the business you are planning to be a part of. Do not open a retail store if all your experience is in car repair for example.

A couple other things to remember. You should know about all the training the parent company offers, the financial stability of the company, and how they have assisted with other franchisees prior to committing and money to it. By researching all of this ahead of time, you should have a pretty good idea how well your business will do in the future. By choosing a stable company that offers a lot of benefits to their franchise owners, you can be sure that your business will be one of the better supported companies in your area.

Always remember that success does not necessarily depend on the franchise itself. It will definitely depend on your attitude, customer experience, and sales abilities. Another thing to keep in mind is that everyday will not be smooth sailing with great sales. Expect some small losses from time to time and learn how to deal with the ebb and flow of daily business. After several positive years as a franchise owner, you should be able to reap the financial rewards of your hard work and dedication.

Financial Freedom and Independence From Home

For those of us that do not have a large amount of capital sitting in the bank, we are going to have to build our own business from the ground up. Fortunately for you, I happen to know a guy that did just exactly that.

We all want financial freedom. Life would be fantastic if we could all afford to travel, enjoy the luxuries in life, and not worry about how we are going to pay next month's bills. Gaining financial independence through a home based business is another method that thousands of people have used to get ahead in life.

Statistically, a majority of people will hold multiple jobs over their lifetime. In most cases, even after earning your degree, or finding your calling in life, you will still change employers 3-4 times. When you factor in the possibility of corporate mismanagement, downsizing, and restructuring, then your financial future begins to look a little cloudy. What all these fancy terms really mean is that you are out of job and must look for another position at another company.

Starting your own business and making it successful provides independence from the corporate rat race, and often provides financial freedom for the owner. Many owners will have the financial ability to pursue other interests and hobbies in their life because they work for themselves. When you are part of a large corporation, you have built in job security. If you are a good worker, you can usually move to a different job within the same company when things get restructured. This is simply not possible when running your own small business. There is not another job, and nowhere to hide, when you work for yourself. If you are going to have your own business, you must focus on generating sales and getting new customers.

To be brutally honest, opening up your own small business is considerably harder than opening a franchise. To start with, you do not have a marketable product or service in the beginning. You do not have a reputable brand that has a track record with consumers. At the early stages of building a business, you do not have a reputation, good or bad.

If you are intent on opening your own small business, a marketable product or service is imperative to get it off the ground. In order to make yourself stand out against the competition, your product or service must do something that no one else does currently. You can certainly open a retail store with a variety of products, but without unique products or services, you will not be able to distinguish yourself from the competition.

As an example, think about the burger business. In most towns across America you can find a Burger King, McDonald's, and Wendy's within driving distance of each other. Even though all three of these companies offer the same product, a burger, they each have their own unique spin to make it different from the others. Would you like that flame broiled, fresh and never frozen, or grilled?

When you are opening your own business, you do not have a reputable brand name to stand behind. This poses a lot of problems from a marketing and advertising perspective. If the customer does not know you, and has no idea what you stand for, how can you ask them to spend their hard-earned money on your product or service?

To continue on that same train of thought, businesses that start from the ground up do not have a reputation to manage either. You cannot manage your reputation, because no one knows who you are. It will take substantial marketing and advertising dollars in order to get your brand name recognized in the community.

Now that you have been given a basic education on the difficulties of starting your own business from the ground up, you can see why it is much easier to choose a franchise. But let's say your dreams do not involve a franchise, and you have your own ideas. What are you supposed to do?

The combination of marketing, advertising, and sales is crucial to the success of your new business. If your business dreams require owning your own company, and selling an unique product or service, then you or someone you hire is going to have to become a pretty good salesperson.

At this point in the book, we are going to assume that you

have a basic idea for your company. Your business should have a fantastic product or service that it is going to sell to other people. If you have not created your own business yet, then Chapter 5, The Basics of Sales, will not be beneficial to you at this time.

I do want to note that it is completely acceptable to go ahead and read through the next chapter so that you feel the continuity of the material being presented. Be sure to come back to chapter 5 as a reference point once your company has established a product or service that it is going to sell.

CHAPTER 5
THE BASICS OF SALES

It doesn't matter what type of business you are going to be in at this point. Someway, somehow, you are going to have to be a salesperson promoting your service or product. In reality, we are all already being sold something everyday.

Think about the old saying, "Would you like fries with that?" Did you know that with just that one single line McDonald's added millions of french fry orders to their sales? It's a constant theme in business: meet the customer's needs, and then try to up-sell them something with their order.

The secret to sales is mastering the basics first, then honing your approach to match your specific industry or niche. You can not sell dentists the same way that you sell tools on construction sites. The basics are all the same, but the pitch has to change in order to be relevant to your end user.

Sales can also be a tricky business. In order to be a successful salesperson, everything has to go correctly a majority of the time.

According to Tom Hopkins, author of the book, *How to Master the Art of Selling*, there are seven selling basics you must master before you can begin selling. I am going to break each part of this down in detail as it is imperative to master the basics of sales before it can be applied to any unique occupation.

The 7 Basic Steps of Sales

1. Prospecting

To most salespeople this is the dirtiest word of the sales process. Prospecting implies that you must go out and search for the customer, often without assistance from the company you work for/with. Many companies use mailers, cold calling, or public databases to come up with a list of potential "prospects" to sell to. This process is becoming outdated with modern technology however. Door-to-door sales and cold calling are almost non-existent anymore. Why is this so? Both door-to-door sales and cold calling are ineffective at turning a prospect into a qualified prospect.

2. Making Contacts

If you are going to make it in any sales profession, you must learn to network. A good contact works with their customer and sells them in a professional manner. Then, when the conversation changes to a project that they can not handle, or their company has no expertise with, that contact often recommends another professional to work with. You want to be that other professional that gets recommended by others.

3. Qualification

Qualifying is by far why most people fail to make it in the sales field. Finding prospects is an easy task; finding qualified prospects is much harder. Unfortunately, your prospect list can be absolutely useless if that person is not a qualified prospect. Let me ask you this. Is the replacement window guy ever found in the new sub-division? Of course not.

4. Presentation

Now your sales process has gotten very personal. Once you have spent all your time prospecting, contacting, and qualifying, your sales pitch will either make or break the sale. Most people believe the presentation is a completely visual and audible transaction. Your customer is judging **ALL** aspects of your presentation, including you personally.

5. Handling Objections

Your sales pitch will never be a 100% closer. Never. Once you have an interested customer, it is imperative that you handle all their questions and concerns with care. This is a major tipping point in the sales process. Listen and clarify before talking.

6. Closing

Now we go to the desk or the credit card comes out. Closing involves all the details of the transaction, such as the 5 W's; who, what, when, where, and why (or how).

7. Referrals

If you have won the customer over, and they are truly satisfied with the products and services received, you have earned the right to ask for a referral. This is one of the easiest sales to make because a friend or family member has already sold them on you and your product or service.

In the game of mattress sales, where I spent 5 1/2 years selling mattresses to consumers, there is no prospecting. Customers came into the store because the company I was working for has advertised to them in some capacity. It might be road signs, newspaper ads, TV ads, or even social media buys. In some manner, that customer heard about the mattress store I was sitting in. I did not have to go out and find them first.

If you are starting a business from scratch, you have to really clarify who your end user is. You can be the best salesperson in the world, but pitching to the wrong person, or someone who will never use your product or service, is a guaranteed fail every time. Look at your biggest competitors and figure out who they are targeting with their advertising. Write down key words and phrases they use, along with any notes on really good marketing techniques they use.

I would suggest that you utilize marketing and advertising as your best friends when staring a business. This does not have to be very expensive however. There are many methods of attracting customers and the scope and breadth of that subject is way too big for this book to cover in any detail.

I do want to take a second and make a special note about marketing and advertising however. As a general rule, word-of-mouth advertising is always the best option. As a business owner, you will learn to love when a customer of yours refers you someone else via a simple conversation.

If your business requires a much larger scale of advertising, then it is important that you learn a term called return on investment, or ROI. Return on investment is a business term that allows you to measure how effective your marketing and advertising dollars are being spent. For most small businesses, radio and television advertising are much too expensive. You will most likely receive better qualified leads and prospects by utilizing social media, word-of-mouth advertising, and small, targeted advertising in appropriate magazines and newspapers.

A savvy business owner should also make attempts at building a relationship outside of your regular prospects. If you were in the mattress business, real estate agents and chiropractors are just a couple examples of relationships worth pursuing. Their clients will have a need for better bedding. Sometimes the timing of these referrals may be months or even years from when you set your network in place. These referrals will never be a consistent source of income, but it should lead to sales that are pleasant surprises in your pay from time to time. Your time is <u>never wasted</u> trying to network and connect with someone that may bring you more sales.

If you have been prospecting and qualifying your contacts, then the warm body in front of you <u>should now be</u> a qualified prospect. Make sure that this person is the decision maker and can pull the trigger on what you are selling. This should be a genuine opportunity to sell something. I am not saying that you are closing every opportunity here, I am saying that your mindset should be that this is "the absolute best" opportunity for this business or person you are talking to to purchase from you.

Now that we have established that you are not going to land a billion customers by prospecting, and that building a small referral network is not going to ensure financial freedom, we have to talk about presenting to your qualified prospect. The sales presentation will make or break a sale faster than anything else that happens. It is critical to appear knowledgeable and confident while interacting with the customer. The pitch, as it is known, must be polished and tested.

In <u>Mattress Buying 101</u>, I talked about the seven things that every customer expects from their salesperson. I believe this is worth repeating here so that every salesperson can make sure their presentation includes all of these points prior to the customer ending the interaction. You as the salesperson must now change your mindset to believe that you will <u>never</u> get this opportunity again, so giving them the best presentation and experience is critical to your success.

Seven Things A Salesperson Must Do

- <u>The salesperson must make a good first impression on you</u>.

Yes, it all truly starts with the greeting. A number of consumers specifically cited the greeting as an important part of the shopping experience. Too often consumers received no greeting at all, which started the shopping experience off on a sour note.

- <u>The salesperson must be knowledgeable</u>.

This probably comes as no great revelation, but it's a reminder that consumers are looking for answers to their questions, and it underscores the need sales associates to spend the time to learn the ins and outs of their product and service. If a salesperson can not answer basic questions about your product or service it is time to let them go. They must be able to explain product differences to the customer inside and out. This is where the selling process begins. Most consumers simply don't know and want to be informed.

- <u>The salesperson must be friendly</u>.

Again, this may not seem to be a great revelation, but there's no doubt that consumers are looking for a friendly face. People like to buy from people they like. A smile can go a long way toward helping your customer relax.

- <u>The salesperson must give the consumer time and space to shop</u>.

This comes up again and again in the consumer research. If they are shopping with their spouse, customers want a chance to talk about what they are seeing, without having a salesperson hanging on their every word. Make sure your salesperson respects boundaries of space and time. The professional sales associate will give the consumer space, but is ready to re-engage with them when needed.

- <u>The salesperson must be concerned about their customer's needs</u>.

Focusing on meeting the consumer's needs establishes a bond of trust that goes a long way in closing the sale.

- <u>The salesperson must keep the atmosphere relaxed</u>.

Consumers say over and over again they don't want high-pressure sale tactics. Keep it relaxed, they say. This can be a challenge. Sales associates may be tempted to do whatever they can to close the sale. But that's a big mistake, according to consumers. They must be ready and able to answer consumers' questions. They lose faith in the salesperson when he or she has to ask someone else for the answer. They must not hover around them.

- <u>The salesperson must deliver a positive shopping experience.</u>

In other words, the smart retail sales associate must excel at each step of the sales process, from a good greeting, to giving the consumer space, to listening to her concerns, and to helping him/her.

Making sure that you implement these seven steps into your presentation gives the customer everything they are looking for. This leads to more sales because you, the salesperson, are creating fewer objections for the customer to be concerned about after the pitch. It is almost as if the customer has handed you a blueprint and said, "here is what I want from you."

Think about a typical sale for a moment and how to incorporate the seven steps into your sales presentation. Below is an example of how the conversation should go. I will use my mattress sales background as the example here.

"Hello! Welcome to Donnie's Mattress Store, how may I assist you today?"

"Oh, Hi. I wanted to see that bed on TV with the wine glass commercial."

"OK. No problem. I have a full selection of Tempurpedic mattresses right over here to show you. May I ask what has you in the market for a new bed?"

"Well, my back has been sore for a little while now, and I guess it's time to replace my old bed."

"Sure, I can certainly understand not wanting to wake up sore and stiff in the morning. Is there any specific reason for the back pain? Herniated or bulging disk maybe?"

"No. It just hurts... especially in the morning after laying in the bed all night. I get a lot a pain and discomfort in my lower back. right here."

"I see. And is there anything else that inhibits your sleep?

Do you have any medical conditions or sleeping issues that make it difficult for you to get a good nights rest?"

"No, not really. I guess it just has to do with getting older."

At this point we have checked off several of the things that are on the list of Seven Things A Salesperson Must Do. Not only did we make a good impression by offering a warm, sincere greeting, but we also proved to be knowledgeable by understanding the wine glass commercial to be Tempurpedic. One of the things that made me really successful on the sales floor was taking the time to sit down with the customer at this point and talk to them about their needs.

In our example, we are also asking the customer about medical issues or sleeping issues as a prompt to get them to open up a bit about their needs. Not only is it a great sales technique to get people to openly talk about themselves, but customers will remember how much you cared about helping them find the right product for their situation. We can check off #3 and #5 now as well. We do care about our customers health and well-being and we are also taking enough time to talk about their needs prior to unloading a sales pitch on them.

Let's go back to our example and continue with our customer.

"I am so sorry. We just started talking and I didn't catch your name. I am Donnie, by the way."

"Hi Donnie, nice to meet you. I am Amber."

"Okay Amber, it is really nice to meet you. In front of me is our entire collection of Tempurpedic mattresses. Do you prefer the top layer of the mattress to feel firmer or softer on your back?"

Once Amber answered this question, we can now start to back off from the sales pitch and give her space. This allows the sales floor to feel relaxed and offers her a positive impression of myself and the company. Ideally she will feel comfortable enough with me to lay down for 5-7 minutes on a new mattress. Prior to her laying down, however, I want to take the time to give her a small education on what she should be looking for.

"A softer feel on top? Sure. Let's try the Tempurpedic Cloud Supreme then. Now before you lie down, we need to address the issues of comfort and support."

"Comfort and support?" Amber asks with her head tilted sideways.

"Yes. Most people come to see me when they have a situation at home with their old bed. They start to wake up feeling sore and stiff in the shoulders, hips, or lower back. This is because the old bed no longer offers comfort and support to your body."

"Okay..."

"Support means that they bed is cradling you so that your spine is aligned from neck to tailbone. Comfort means that the bed has enough layers of foam on top to cushion your back and joints. This will allow you to stay in one position longer while sleeping. Having both of these in the new bed will help you get your best night's sleep."

There are two things going on simultaneously here during our presentation. One, we are educating the customer about how to properly purchase a mattress. Second, we are building trust and confidence through our sales presentation. At no point have we had to put on the "hard sale" or attempted to "close 'em fast". Your customer deserves a much better presentation than that.

Now is the perfect time to offer space and keep the relaxed atmosphere. Changing any part of the sales process right now could be detrimental to making the sale. Why? This is clearly the most uncomfortable part for the customer.

Not only are you asking the customer to make a decision right this second, but you have bombarded them with information. Now is the time to leave a positive shopping experience by offering support and clarity. Offer to explain anything that needs clarification and support your argument for why they should be buying and dealing with you. If your price is higher than the competition, let them know why you are different. Having a higher price is not always a deal breaker for people.

Most importantly, do not change tone or attitude during the support phase. Walk them through everything slowly and confidently. Ease their mind about the change of vendors or supplier issues. Make sure you repeat the advantages of dealing with you and your company.

I truly believe that if you follow the list of sales techniques I have outlined here you will win more customers over on a consistent basis. I used these techniques to make a lot of money as a mattress salesperson and store manager for Sleepy's, but the general principles of these techniques will apply in any field or business setting. Additionally, you will find that you will have fewer customer complaints about your service or product because it was fully explained in detail.

Now it's time to get you mentally and financially prepared to grow your business and wallet!

CHAPTER 6
TIME TO RESET

So now that we have worked through a couple different personal finance and business concepts, it is time to get ready to build true wealth. In order to do this though, we have to evaluate where we are and "reset" our mental and financial base in order to build upon it.

How do you build a house? Do you build the attic first and go down? Of course not. Your foundation for growth requires us to mentally clear the building lot and set the foundation first.

I already asked you to investigate and create a business. Did you do it yet? If you have not begun working on this vital step, then I am asking you to put the book down and do not advance your reading at this point. We can not begin building your foundation without it.

Below are the 4 simple steps to "reset" your life for personal growth and wealth accumulation. Please do not try to skip over this part, or come back and get it later. All of these things have to be in order for you to move forward in your journey. I would not waste your time talking about something I did not truly believe to be important.

Time to Reset:

- ALL credit card and consumer loan debt eliminated
- ALL auto, boat, and plane loan debt eliminated
- Current on any and all other debts (such as student loans and mortgages)
- Business created within your home state, licensed and insured (if necessary)

It's now time to build your first budget!

With the current state of the working world, it is best for both your personal life and your future business plans to be as lean financially as you can get. Some people call it being financially conservative, others will call it frugal or cheap. I will just call it intelligent. You now know better than making these mistakes, and you have been taught better at this point too.

Creating and implementing a budget can assist in helping you, as a consumer, cut unnecessary spending. Utilizing a budget will help eliminate any financial pain caused by unforeseen financial disasters as well. You will be able to save money for future economic hardships and bad times. You will be able to retire with dignity, and you will be able to grow a small business.

One of the most important elements of creating a budget is establishing a baseline for what expenses you actually have every month. Get together all phone bills, car bills, groceries, or utilities that must be paid every month. You'll also want to include bills that will change monthly as well. In the first few months of a budget you might have to take an educated guess, but as time progresses you will be able to make a more accurate and efficient assessment. This will give you a basic, rudimentary knowledge of where your pay check is going every month.

The next step is to identify all the sources of your income. Do you receive any child support? Do you receive money anywhere outside the confines of your regular employment? Any additional funds that you receive each month should to be clearly listed and in the budget just as any conventional source of income would be.

Now that you have counted how much money you make and spend each month, you then need to evaluate how you are actually spending your money. Evaluating where your money goes each month helps to show trends in spending that you might not even be conscious of. Are you eating out too often? Are you spending a great deal of money on coffee every morning? It's very easy to lose track of just how much money you are spending on things you don't truly need.

Once you have been able to establish your income, expenses, and have set up a budget, then it is time to plan your goals. As I already discussed, our first plan of attack is to eliminate all credit card debt, consumer loans, and all automobile debts as well. Please also make sure that you are current on any and all other debts such as student loans and the mortgage for your primary residence. Additionally, any outstanding medical bills or other payment plans need to be eliminated at this time.

The only two acceptable debts to carry at this point are a mortgage and any student loan debts. We are going to attack those a little bit later on.

Your second goal should now be to establish an emergency fund of 3 to 6 months worth of expenses. Please make a note that we were talking about expenses only at this point. If your monthly expenses totaled $2,000, then your emergency fund should be between $6,000 and $12,000.

Having covered the basics of budgeting, I am now also providing a link for you to download an excel budget template for free. I believe it is an awesome tool to help turn your life around financially. At this point, it is time to turn our attention to the emergency fund and why you need it in the first place.

What is an emergency fund? Do I really need one?

Personal finance advisers seem to always provide us with a couple of generic phrases about what we should be doing to secure our future. One of those generic phrases is called an "emergency fund". Most advisers seem to agree that the first thing you should concern yourself with, after meeting the basic living expenses of course, is to create an emergency fund for life's mess ups. This account should consist of liquid cash money that is quickly accessible in the event of a financial crisis. Examples of financial emergencies include job loss, sudden illness, and unexpected home repair/housing costs.

The purpose of an emergency fund is to upgrade your financial security so that you can meet sudden unexpected expenses during an emergency. At the same time your new emergency fund should reduce your reliance on credit cards. You should not use the fund to buy a car or take a vacation. You should use it only in the case of true emergencies.

We will all have to face financial emergencies of different degrees in our life, but a person prepared with a good emergency fund will definitely handle the situation better than someone that does not have one at all. You may feel that with your current financial situation you cannot afford to create an emergency fund, but the harder truth is that you cannot afford to get caught without one.

How much money should we keep in an emergency fund?

The length of your emergency fund is ultimately up to you. Three months of expenses is the absolute minimum amount of cash allowed in an emergency fund. Six months of expenses is preferred for families with children. If you are in a situation where your employment is quite secure, or you work for yourself, then three months of expenses might be adequate. Additionally, if you are in a high demand field, or are highly trained within your field, then three months is probably adequate as well.

If your employment is less secure, or you do not have any highly qualified skills, then your goal should be six months of expenses in an emergency fund. Specifically, if your income is relatively high versus your peers within the same industry then you need to be extra cautious. For example, a restaurant manager that makes $60,000 per year in a field where the average salary is $48,000 per year should have six months worth of expenses in their emergency fund.

Larger families and couples with children should always consider having closer to six months worth of expenses on hand as well. In a single-parent household, or a household with two parents and only one works full-time, there should never be less than a six month emergency fund.

How do I save money for my emergency fund?

Start small. The key to starting any new task is to start small and do not ever believe your end goal is impossible. If you do not have an emergency fund currently and find it difficult to save income every month, try placing small amounts in your savings account everyday. Even something as small as $1 per day will add up over time. Remember, accumulating 3-6 months of living expenses is going to take time to accomplish.

Start early. If you are relatively young, and do not have a family yet, this is the best time to start saving money for your emergency fund. You should be able to save a considerable amount now, as you do not have other people to plan for yet. It is a good idea to start early as your emergency fund will also need to grow along with your expenses in life.

Be regular. Try to save small amount of money every day, week, or month and be consistent about it. Consistency is the key to growing your emergency fund. Get into the habit of saving a fixed amount of money on a regular basis. Stick to the biweekly schedule when you get paid or a monthly interval if that works better for you. You can even use automatic payroll deductions so that a fixed amount of money will be moved automatically to your emergency fund bank account.

Every little bit adds up. Begin cutting back on any unnecessary extras and try to put some part of any other income, such as tax refunds or product rebates, into your emergency fund account. You should also be excited to see just how fast adjusting your spending will increase your savings. Placing any amount in your fund, whether it be daily, weekly, or monthly is a positive step forward. Remember, even some small amount is better than nothing at all.

Make it a habit. It is always difficult to start something new, but once you get into the habit of saving even small amounts in your emergency fund, you will begin to get used to doing it all the time. Once you have gotten comfortable with the routine and have a track record of timely deposits, gradually try to increase the amount you are saving up to 20% of your income. Do not touch your fund for anything other than a true emergency, no matter the temptation. A real emergency is something that could not be foreseen or planned for.

Where do I keep my emergency fund?

At first, you should start saving a small amount of money in a plain old savings account that can be accessed quickly in an emergency. When you have saved a considerable amount of money, or you have reached your goal of 6 months expenses, keep half of the money liquid at the bank and the other half of it should go where you can get a higher interest rate, like a money market account. Under no circumstances should your emergency fund be invested in the stock market. This should remain liquid and quickly accessible at all times.

My definition of accessible funds is really quite simple. For me personally, accessibility means that I should be able to access my entire emergency fund (both halves) within 48 hours.

Once you start saving money for your emergency fund you should start to feel more relaxed, confident and less stressed about your future. Watching the balance in your account grow every month should give you a sense of pride and satisfaction. You should be proud of the progress you are making. Celebrate when you reach mini goals such as one months expenses, two months, etc. You are now well on your way in getting prepared to handle any unforeseen financial crisis.

It's Time To Hustle

Once you have achieved your goal of paying down all your bad debts, and have an emergency fund going, it's really important that you begin to focus some of your time, effort, and energy on building your own small business.

We have previously talked about wealth being obtained through a combination of hard work, smart investments, and owning your own business. I think it's really important to stress that all four of these things must occur in order for you to succeed once you have reset your life.

I don't think it's important to spend any time talking about hard work. Most people I know do work hard. In fact, a lot of people work much harder than I do. It's almost a badge of honor in America to work harder and longer hours than someone else.

Unfortunately, hard work alone does not equate to financial success. If it did, then police officers, teachers, firefighters, and military veterans would be some of the wealthiest people in America today. Reality tells us that hard work is only one part of the equation.

In the next two chapters of the book, where going to discuss in detail the basics of investing, and real estate and business loans. Both of these are going to be instrumental chapters in your quest to build wealth going forward. But right now, I would like to spend some time telling you why it is so important to start your own business and I have some income coming in from somewhere else other than your primary job.

We spent a lot of time earlier in the book discussing inflation, and the effects that it has on the average person's wage as well. I can tell you for a fact that most people are not making more money than they did before. In fact, 1950s and early 1960s America was based on a one income household. In today's society, mom and dad both work, and sometimes relatives live in the same household in order to afford all the bills.

I hope at this point that you trust me enough to tell you that it's not your fault. There is nothing wrong with you as a person, and there is most certainly nothing wrong with how hard you work. The bigger problem is that manufacturing jobs simply do not exist in America today, and thus wages have become depressed as we switched to a service based economy.

There are many people that are much smarter than me in the world. They have the ability to discuss all of these factors in intimate detail. I am sure there are Harvard and Yale educated economists telling anyone who will listen that a service-based economy is a natural progression forward. I simply don't understand how this can be true to the average person.

Please tell me how you can look a parent in the eye, and tell them that they are better off now that both parents have to work full-time in order to make ends meet. How can you honestly tell people that replacing high-quality manufacturing jobs with lower paying service jobs is a progression forward?

I sincerely hope at this point that I have shared enough information with you so that you can see you are not to blame for the situation that you are in. My biggest concern now, is that no one else is going to help you out of the mess.

In other words, you're going to have to start working for yourself. If you would truly like an opportunity to enjoy a better quality life, then you must learn to become dependent upon yourself for your income. There are a multitude of ways to do this, and were going to talk about some of them, passive income included, in another section.

Right now I need you to understand how important your own small business is going to be to your financial future. It may seem a really small and insignificant piece of the puzzle as you read this, but your small business is going to grow into something that can produce income for you and your family down the road. Remember, I started my journey with just one small book on mattresses. That has since transformed into revenue streams from book sales, website ad revenue, and business and consultation income.

When I started my small business, the Masters Investment Group, I never had plans of even advertising the business to the general public. I originally created the business so that I could invest in business opportunities that an individual investor could not. I had no idea it would grow into what it is becoming now.

The much larger point is that your small business will become something more than you think it will be down the road. It will become larger and produce more income than you can imagine at some point. It is imperative that it is set up as part of your journey going forward.

CHAPTER 7
THE BASICS OF INVESTING

At this point I have already discussed how most millionaires became successful through a combination of work, owning a business, and investing in the stock market and owning real estate. Maybe your goal is not to be a millionaire, maybe it is just to retire with dignity and class. That is perfectly fine.

Before you begin this chapter on investing, you should have completed all the prior steps outlined. At this point, you should have eliminated all credit card, consumer, and automobile debts. You should also have a liquid and accessible emergency fund of 3 to 6 months worth of expenses. The only two loans that are acceptable to have at this point in the process are student loans (even though they are not good debt) and your home mortgage.

Ideally, paying off your other debts and adding that side hustle has freed up enough cash to start paying off your student loans and your home mortgage aggressively. The idea behind the budget is that once you have eliminated your other debts, you can then then begin to snowball that money towards your two remaining loans or using that money to grow your business if you are having some early success.

Thus far in the book we have covered the subjects of education and work, as well as owning a business. The next logical step is to prepare for retirement. One thing we know for sure is that the stock market is going to have to help you get there.

If you are interested in the basics of the stock market, then you are already on the right track. Before you open a trading account though, you should know exactly what you are getting yourself into. Remember, anything that involves large sums of money needs to be taken seriously and with the proper preparation.

So what are the stock market basics that every investor should know? Where should we begin in a world that is often complex and misunderstood?

Just as with most financial subjects, many investors are given general guidance as it pertains to investing. Most investors are told to contribute to their retirement account. Many people have offered financial advice such as contribute 10% of your earnings to your retirement.

In order to understand investing at any level, you have to understand your own personal goals and why you are willing to take a risk on nothing but electronic wishes. For me personally, there are three criteria to consider when making any investment, not just the stock market. The three most important criteria to me are, preservation of capital, expected return, and loss of opportunity.

I would like to take a moment and break each of those down for you now. I feel it is extremely important to understand investing in general before you can begin to understand the stock market.

The most important rule of investing in anything should be the ability to preserve capital. What this means is that by taking the risk of investing my money in something, I should be able to reduce or remove the risk of losing my initial investment.

For example, let's say that I have already gone through all the steps mentioned previously, including having an emergency fund, and I now have an extra $200 per month to begin investing with. My first priority should always be to preserve that $200 per month.

So now I have been able to save that $200 per month for the past year I now have $2400 available to invest with. What is my new goal? My goal is the same as before. Preserve the $2400 that I have been able to save thus far.

Now if our only goal is to assume zero risk and make sure that that $2400 is preserved at this point next year, there are only two places that I can invest that money to be sure that it is still there intact in 12 months. One of those investment options is a bank account, the other is a certificate of deposit. Either way my expected return is approximately 1 to 2% over the next 12 months. In other words, I can expect to put up my $2400 and receive my $2400 back, plus $24- 48 in interest 12 months from now.

Now that you have been educated about finance, you understand that you cannot out save inflation. Therefore, you understand that getting a 1% return on your money over the long term is not going to improve your financial situation or help generate long-term wealth for your retirement.

This is where the next stage of investing comes in, or expected return. In order to make more than 1% interest on my money, I have to be willing to assume some risk. What this means is that I am giving up some of the control of my capital in exchange for an expected return that is higher than the 1% available at bank accounts and certificate of deposits.

This is where most people fail to understand investing. There is a constant risk and reward scenario for every type of investment that you will make in your lifetime. This particularly includes the stock market. In order to make an average gain of approximately 6 to 8% on your money year after year, you must be willing to take the risk to lose some of your initial capital.

The good news is that with proper money management and smart investing decisions, your gains can truly be unlimited. The bad news is that by taking excessive risk you can lose all of your capital. Please don't worry, by the end of this chapter you will be smarter than that.

Finally, when it comes to investing there is also the loss of opportunity to be considered. In other words, by using the $2400 that I have saved over the past year and investing it in a particular investment, what opportunities will I lose? For example, what if I invested in Hewlett-Packard and missed out on investing in the next Apple?

The loss of opportunity is not to be taken lightly. It is very easy to put your head down and focus on one thing at a time, never realizing that another opportunity is staring you right in the face. An example of this would be tying up all of your extra money in the stock market and not being able to partake in a great real estate investment opportunity.

So there you have it. The three most important aspects of investing are preservation of capital, expected return, and loss of opportunity. But what in the world does all of this have to do with the stock market specifically? Quite a bit.

Before we begin using any of the technical jargon, we need to clarify some common myths that surround the stock market in general.

The first myth that many people believe about the stock market is that stocks are expensive. What most people do not know, however, is that stocks vary in price greatly. Some stocks trade for fractions of a penny, and others will trade for thousands of dollars per share.

Stocks that trade for five dollars per share or less are commonly referred to as penny stocks. Penny stocks tend to be companies that are experiencing difficult times. In most cases, they have little to no profit and are experiencing problems financing and growing their business. Penny stocks are highly speculative (read super risky), and should never be considered an investment.

The second myth that is taught about the stock market is that the returns can be mind blowing. It is actually quite common to see advertisements on the TV, Internet, and radio touting amazing returns by investing in a particular stock or with a certain company.

In some cases, it has been possible to invest as little as $1000 in a stock and 20 years later have that investment be worth millions. Unfortunately for us all, those returns are the exceptions not the norm. In general, taking on the risk of investing in the stock market should allow you returns that are 2 to 3 times that of inflation. In other words, if inflation is averaging 1.5 to 2% per year, then your stock market investments should be returning 4.5 to 6% per year or higher.

For many people, they do not believe the risk of investing in the stock market is worth the return. But everything that we do requires a certain amount of risk. If your plan is to build wealth long-term, and ours is, then you must be confident in using the stock market as part of your retirement. So logically, the next question is, how do we do that?

Purchasing stock is as simple as buying a pair of shoes. For example, let's say you go to the store and you are given a selection of 10 pairs of shoes with the exact same colors and the exact same design. However, upon closer inspection, some shoes are priced cheaper while some of the other shoes are more expensive. In this scenario, you would choose the cheaper shoes because it is nothing but the price that makes them different from one another.

Let's now assume that all of the shoes have the same price, same color, and same design, but some of the shoes will last longer because they have clearly been made better, with better material. In this example, you would likely choose the shoes that you could wear for a longer period of time, as long as the price was the same. This exact scenario is represented almost every day in the stock market.

Every time we purchase a stock, we set out to choose the best stock available. How that stock is priced versus its competition determines whether or not that stock is expensive or cheap.

Once you have decided upon a sector of the market that you would like to invest in, you should then consider all the stocks within that sector. As an easy example, let's stick with shoes. Do you want to invest in Nike, Adidas, or Under Armour?

The largest problem with trying to select an individual stock is that no one knows what the company will do in the future. One of my favorite expressions is often used on Wall Street. "Past performance is not indicative of future returns."

In other words, just because a company has grown faster than its competition previously, that is no indication that it will continue to do so going forward. Unless you are highly trained, or highly educated, I do not suggest trying to pick individual stocks. You are much better off selecting mutual funds or ETF's.

Mutual funds and ETF's each have their own advantages and disadvantages. I personally recommend that people purchase exchange traded funds. ETF, or exchange traded fund, is an umbrella of stocks or bonds that trade on the stock market at a set price. Just like any other common stock, ETF's are bought and sold based upon supply and demand. Exchange traded funds are an umbrella of stocks, not just one specific company. For example, there is most likely an ETF that owns shares of Nike, Adidas, and Under Armour as well as many other apparel manufacturers. By investing in an umbrella of companies, you are reducing the risk of being wrong about the prospect of one specific company. Rather, you are investing based upon the prospect of a sector at large.

Think of it this way. Let's say that the economy is doing well, and people are spending more disposable income. From an investing standpoint, you believe that this means clothing, sports apparel, and high-end shoes will sell faster than before. At this point you have done your research, and you have found an ETF with the stock symbol SHOE.

SHOE owns an equal amount of Nike, Adidas, and Under Armour. By placing your investment in this specific ETF, you are betting on the sector, or group of companies in a similar business, to do well.

ETF's have been traded in the US since 1993. Initially, ETF's were not available to the individual investor. Rather, they were used by financial institutions or institutional investors trying to diversify their risk by selecting specific sectors, not individual stocks.

Mutual funds have been in existence since 1924 in the United States. Serving the average investor for decades, they are known to have been established since 1924, but not commonly purchased by individuals until the 1970's. Similar to the ETF, a mutual fund consists of a basket of investments designed to reflect the performance of its holdings. The way these securities are bought and sold is one area where there is a major difference between ETF's and mutual funds.

ETF's share a lot of similar characteristics to stocks as it pertains to trading. The share price of an ETF fluctuates throughout the day while the markets are open. This allows an investor to trade continually throughout the day. Mutual funds and index funds are traded throughout the day as well, however their price is based on the closing price of the day before.

Another marked difference between ETF's and mutual funds is the fee structure of both. ETF's tend to be very transparent and have a straightforward expense ratio, while mutual funds may employ a number of different ways to charge an investor. ETF's tend to have a few advantages over mutual funds. Some of those advantages include lower ownership costs, tax advantages, liquidity of trading, no minimum investment requirement, and many more.

There are a few disadvantages to ETF's as well. For instance, your trading fees will vary widely among stockbrokers. Additionally, there could also be sudden price changes as the ETF is traded openly throughout the trading day.

So What Is The Big Difference Between ETF's, Stocks, and Mutual Funds Then?

ETF's have many similarities to stocks

- They are considered investments

- They are bought and sold on a stock exchange

- They can be traded during trading hours

- Their prices can change through the day

- They are purchased through brokerage accounts

ETF's also have many differences from stocks

- They consist of multiple, different securities

- They offer greater diversification than just one single stock

- You can invest your entire portfolio in just one ETF

- They often have less volatility than single stocks

ETF's: The Alternative to Mutual Funds

At this point, it is probably a fair question to ask why ETF's are the better alternative to mutual funds? I have highlighted some of the reasons I believe ETF's are better below.

Mutual funds always offer a stable price. At the end of the trading day, the net asset value is calculated, or NAV. As it pertains to market timing, there can be a large difference between the current market price and the end of the day net asset value for a mutual fund. What this means, is that when you go to purchase the mutual fund you may receive more or less shares based on the NAV at the end of the trading day. This is not the case for ETF's however. As the trading day progresses, ETF's offer a real-time price quote so that the quote you are given is the price you would pay to execute the trade at that specific moment.

Over a long period of time, the performance of ETF's should be slightly better than mutual funds. This is because of the previously mentioned fees that are charged to manage a mutual fund. ETF's tend to have lower fees, therefore over a longer period of time their performance should be better.

ETF shareholders also get to decide when they are buying or selling an ETF. This offers you the opportunity for better tax efficiency. In other words, you can buy or sell an ETF as needed so that you control whether your capital gains are taxed at a short term income level, or long-term income level. When it comes to mutual funds, the fund manager decides when he or she is selling a particular stock. This means that the fund must disclose the sale, and pass along the appropriate short-term or long-term gain.

One of my favorite aspects about trading an ETF, is that there is no minimum investment for the investor. Most mutual funds have a minimum investment amount that you are required to purchase in order to be part of the fund. ETF's on the other hand, allow you to purchase one share or 100,000 shares.

401(K) Retirement Plan Explained

The 401(k) plan makes it easy and convenient for you to save money for your retirement. Once you enroll in your plan, your contributions are automatically deducted from your paycheck before you even get to see it. This automatic savings can be a strict savings discipline, especially if you're not good at saving money.

Since we are planning to pass through the retirement stage of life in style, instead of broke and worried, a 401(k) will be a real advantage when it comes to making your retirement as comfortable as possible. In general, it's much harder to save when you receive a full paycheck without deductions.

There are a couple advantages to a 401(k) plan. First, the contributions that are deducted from your paycheck are not taxed. By not taxing your contributions, you actually pay less tax on your paycheck. Secondly, in most cases, your employer will match at least part of your contribution.

Most 401(k) plans comes with a range of investment options, including stock funds, bond funds, balanced funds, international funds, and some may let you purchase company stock. You must decide how your contributions are distributed among the plan's offerings. You should consider your long-term financial objectives, your tolerance for risk, and how close you are to retirement age when doing so. I do not advise you to take on any extra risk in your portfolio, just because a stock fund is performing really well. It is always best to take a conservative approach, making sure that you are investing your money in many different mutual funds with a long term track record of success (10+ years).

In my opinion, it is best to have a balanced allocation strategy. Yes, you want your returns to be as high as possible over time. At the same time, we also need to preserve and grow our investment. Aim for returns of 8 to 10% per year over a 10 year period for your overall portfolio.

It is critical that you pay close attention and monitor the progress of your 401(k) plan. The plan is required by law to provide you with statements in order to assist you in managing your plan. Depending upon the provider of your 401(k) plan, you may receive monthly or quarterly statements, online or Internet access, and some general investing advice.

Each 401(k) plan provider also specifies when and how you can make changes to your investments. Some plans will allow you to make changes daily, while others will only allow a limited number of transactions per year. Please be aware of the rules concerning your specific plan. No matter what the rules are for changing your investments, you, and only you, responsible for checking on your plan's performance and making any changes. No one other than you can change how your money is allocated inside your plan.

Certain 401(k) plans also allow you gain access to your savings in case of a financial emergency before you reach the age of eligibility. This access to your funds may come via a loan (with interest), or hardship withdrawal. In the case of a hardship withdrawal, you will have to pay ordinary income tax on the amount withdrawn and a 10% penalty to the government. You do not have to pay the penalty if you meet one of the following.

- Purchasing your primary residence

- Avoiding eviction from your current residence

- Paying tuition for yourself, your spouse, your children or dependents

- Paying funeral expenses for a family member

- Medical expenses above 7.5% of your adjusted gross income

While it is true that you can take withdrawals at any age, the withdrawals are not penalty free unless your reason for withdrawal matches one of the five previously outlined criteria. Once you reach the age of 59 1/2 however, all withdrawals from your 401(k) plan are penalty free.

Once you reach the age of 70, you must begin taking distributions by April 1 of the following year. By following our investment advice, hopefully you will not have to withdraw any money before turning 70.

Diversification and Asset Allocation

Having mentioned the terms asset allocation and diversification, I think it is only fair that we spend some time talking about it. So what is a reasonable amount of diversification for your portfolio? In other words, how should we invest our money in order to avoid risk?

Diversification is a very tricky thing to calculate. Ultimately, several factors need to be considered when you talk about diversification. Those factors include how much money you have invested, how much financial knowledge you have, and how much time and effort you plan to spend reviewing your portfolio. All of this will help determine how much diversification is necessary.

Until you begin working for yourself full-time, the only retirement account that most people have access to is a 401(k) plan. Because 401(k) plans are limited in their offerings, most people can only invest in mutual funds and company stock. We already know that investing in a mutual fund offers some diversification.

In most cases, your retirement plan will offer you choices in regards to the mutual funds that you can purchase. There should be a minimum of 20 to 25 funds available for you to invest in, with each fund focusing on a particular section of the stock market. For example, most employers will have mutual funds that will allow you to invest in small cap stocks, mid cap stocks, large cap stocks, international stocks, and bonds. Many of these mutual funds will have investment goals ranging from highly conservative to considerably risky. Again, our advice is to look for funds that have a long term track record of 8 to 10% growth per year.

Initially, it is best to allocate your funds into at least five different mutual funds. If you are a younger person, your allocation should be heavily weighted towards small and mid-cap stocks, as they will offer more growth over time. Once you reach about 40 years of age, your portfolio should begin to balance out equally between small and mid-cap stocks, as well as bonds and high yield funds. Once you reach the age of 55, you need to become much more conservative with your investments. In the case of older people, we recommend that you only focus on high yield funds, as well as bonds.

As time goes on some of your funds would do really well and others will not. You will need to look at your investments on a regular basis. You will also need to re-balance your retirement account from time to time. Re-balancing simply means taking profits in some areas so you can invest more in under-performing areas.

Asset Allocation, Diversification, and Managing Risk

Asset allocation means spreading your investment funds across various asset categories. As an overall investment strategy, asset allocation will help the average investor reduce the overall portfolio risk, volatility, and increase profits. Asset allocation is important to use when designing a portfolio. The goal should never be picking or choosing specific securities, instead your goal should be a general focus on the overall architecture of broad investment categories that will ultimately bring financial independence.

Asset Allocation Basics

The main concept behind asset allocation is that not all investments follow the same cycle. Therefore, you are able to balance out your portfolio based upon the different risk and return cycles. By spreading out your investment dollars among the different asset classes, you would be achieving asset allocation. The different asset classes include stocks, bonds, real estate, commodities, and other assets such as physical gold and silver.

By owning different types of asset classes, you are bringing different levels of risk and return to your overall portfolio. Generally speaking, the different asset classes react differently to different economic conditions. As a general guideline, different asset classes will rise and fall at different times during a market rally or depression.

For example, let's say that you own both investment real estate and equities in the stock market. During a market upturn, the real estate market may begin picking up steam faster than the stock market. By having assets in both, you are achieving asset allocation so that your total portfolio rises. Additionally, the returns of one asset class may be declining which allows you to invest more money while that sector is on "sale". At the same time, another asset class could be growing quickly. This means you are not buying as much with the same amount of money. If you have properly diversified your portfolio to include many different types of assets, as we have recommended, a market downturn should not reek havoc on your portfolio.

Once you have accumulated significant assets, it would be wise to sit down with a financial adviser. A good financial adviser will be able to help you identify the different types of asset classes that would be appropriate for your investment objectives and risk tolerance. Depending upon your age, your investment objectives, and your risk tolerance, a good financial adviser would advise you on the best way to allocate your funds.

The major asset classes

Listed below are the three major asset classes that most people will take advantage of when creating an asset allocation within their stock portfolio.

- Stocks (ETF's and mutual funds included)

- Bonds

- Cash alternatives

Stocks have historically provided investors with a higher than average annual return as compared to bonds and cash alternatives. Because of their potential for higher returns, stocks are typically much more volatile, and carry a greater degree of risk than the other asset classes. Investments in stocks are usually more suitable for those investors that have a long term investment horizon.

In general, bonds have historically been less volatile than stocks. Bonds typically do not provide the opportunity for capital gains that stocks do. However, they could be appropriate, and even highly recommended, for investors that need a fixed and stable income stream from their investments. In addition, bonds carry an interest rate risk. As interest rates rise, bond values tend to fall. When interest rates fall, bond values will generally rise.

In most investment accounts there is the ability to invest in cash alternatives as well. Cash alternatives could be a simple money market account, or a sweep account. No matter the name of this type of account, these accounts do not provide capital appreciation or income potential. They are definitely the least volatile of the three asset classes. Nevertheless, they are subject to inflation risk. These cash alternative accounts are generally highly liquid investments and provide investor with quick and easy access to the funds.

Not only is asset allocation a great tool to make sure that you are diversifying your funds across different asset classes, but each asset class will also allow you to diversify within it. For example, when you choose to invest in stocks, you have the option of investing in micro cap, small cap, large cap, or what are called bellwether stocks. Oftentimes you will also have the ability to divide your funds according to different investment styles. For example, you may decide to invest for growth, for value, or for income. There are certainly an endless combination of investment possibilities, but the objective is always the same. You should be utilizing asset allocation as another method of diversifying your portfolio, and achieving the highest returns for your level of risk.

How to divide your assets

As we have previously stated, the main objective of asset allocation is to design a portfolio that gives you the highest return possible while reducing the amount of risk you are exposed to. One majorly important part of asset allocation is your time horizon. The people that have years until retirement can take higher risks, as there is plenty of time to ride out the ups and downs of the stock market. Those with shorter time frames, need to eliminate risk and accept smaller returns.

A good financial adviser will help you construct a portfolio by factoring in your investment objectives, your risk tolerance, and your investment time frame. Additionally, financial advisers will usually be able to suggest a model portfolio that strikes a balance between your expected risk and return.

If you are like most people, and you don't have the time or expertise to build and manage a diversified portfolio of securities, then you may want to consider investing in what is called a target dated fund. These funds are a special type of mutual fund that offers diversification by buying different asset classes. The fund is managed with a specific investment objective. The objective changes as you get closer to your retirement age. For example, if you have 30 or 40 years until you retire, the funds should be highly aggressive in the stock market. As you get closer to your retirement age however, the same mutual fund will begin to buy bonds and fixed investment securities. By doing this automatically for you, and investor does not have to take the time and effort or energy to track their individual portfolio.

Once you have set up your portfolio, it is important to revisit your entire portfolio on a consistent basis. The main reason for revisiting your portfolio is to make sure that your current investments are still in line with your objectives and goals. You also want to make sure that your investments are keeping pace with the general stock market.

CHAPTER 8
REAL ESTATE AND BUSINESS LOANS

Now that we have already covered mortgages and deeds of trust in great length, I would like to set down some best practices to use when you are in search of a new mortgage for your real estate investments.

Always Look For The Best Mortgage Rates

Whatever you do please don't ever just blindly accept someone's referral when applying for a mortgage through their favorite lender. Many times the advertisement will read something like, "we work closely with this lender". At this point, you should be mentally sharp enough to understand that statement really means, "we are friends, we play golf together, and he always buys the beer". Remember, the person making the referral will not be making the payments every month for the next 30 years, you on the other hand will be.

Mortgage loan officers tend to work off a referral network of real estate agents and builders. They don't necessarily have the most competitive mortgage rates because they have a steady stream of interested people calling them all the time. Make sure you scout around, and try to get the lowest rate. If you would like to work with that preferred lender, approach the loan officer and ask him to match a competing quote. Better yet, ask him to actually beat the quote you were given by someone else! If you decide to just blindly apply for a mortgage without doing your homework, you may pay hundreds or even thousands of dollars more in additional costs and fees.

Always State That You Are Prepared To Apply For A Loan <u>NOW</u>

If you're planning to purchase a home, tell the loan officer that you are rate shopping and that you possess a "ratified contract" to purchase a house. If you are refinancing your mortgage, tell the loan officer that you are ready to apply for a mortgage immediately. If you don't tell the loan officer up front, he may provide a fake quote or a ballpark number.

Loan officers are not stupid. They know that you will most likely talk to several other lenders. The loan officer is expecting you to shop around for a couple days and figures you will call him back in a day or two asking him to match or beat another quote. Also, since mortgage rates change daily and are subject to change at any time in general, the loan officer is not bothered about giving you a fake number to start with. Be especially leery about any loan officer willing to give you a quote without running your credit score to see what you would qualify for.

Ask For The Total Points AND The Total Fees

When calling or working with a mortgage lender, make sure you ask for the total points and the total fees for the loan. Be sure you also ask about any loan origination fees that may apply. If asked, mortgage brokers should mention how they are paid for finding you the best rate.

Some Lenders Do Not Charge A Loan Origination Fee

When you are being given the quote, directly ask the lender if there is an additional loan origination fee or broker fee being charged. Also request a detailed list of every other fee that will appear on the good faith estimate. Make sure any credit report and appraisal fees are clearly listed. It may help to ask the lender to itemize each fee, just so you can see a complete breakdown of any money that you will owe out of pocket.

Don't be discouraged by title fees, attorney fees, or escrow. A lender will estimate these but these charges are not in any way related to the overall cost of your mortgage. In most cases, title fees and attorney fees are not charged by the lender. Title fees and attorney fees are most often paid directly to the people that do that specific task for your mortgage.

Confirm The "Lock-In" Period

Whenever you are purchasing a new property, make sure you specifically request the length of time that your mortgage rate is locked in. Most loans typically take 30 to 45 days to close. A 60 day lock in is usually enough time to allow for any mistakes and errors.

If you should run into a situation where your rate lock in period expires, the lender will have to lock you in at the higher of your original rate or the current rate that's on the market. This situation is a complete loss for the borrower. You never wanna let your rate expire on you.

Never Float The Rate

Remember these words, never float your mortgage rate. Just don't do it. A good mortgage broker will always be able to lock in your rate and points. If the mortgage rates drop, your loan officer should be able to apply all the current information towards a new loan at the lower rate.

Get A Good Faith Estimate A Few Days Before Closing

Make sure to get a copy of the final good faith estimate at least 72 hours before the arranged closing day. Check everything to confirm the mortgage rate, points, fees, and any mortgage insurance premium (if applicable) match what you were told. Make sure that everything on the paper is exactly what you planned for. Ask questions if you don't understand any aspect of the paper work. Demand that any undisclosed fees be discarded and removed immediately. Make sure you get a new estimate if the loan officer agrees to make any changes. You must remember to get everything in writing. The day of your loan closing is way too late to argue over any discrepancies on your new mortgage.

Types Of Real Estate

Residential Real Estate

Residential real estate consists of either a single family or joint family property that is available for non-business purposes. There will be a multitude of different housing types and sizes. The size of real estate is usually measured in square feet.

Commercial Real Estate

Commercial real estate is a property that is designed specifically for business purposes. For instance, commercial real estate could include restaurants, offices, parks, malls, gas stations, and convenience stores.

Industrial Real Estate

Industrial real estate consists of properties that are used for building or manufacturing something. Sometimes the term industrial real estate is also used to encompass a vast range of business types. Most people associate warehouse and/or manufacturing space with industrial real estate.

Real Estate Investment Trust (REIT)

A real estate investment trust, or REIT for short, consist of a basket of properties. Most real estate investment trusts trade on a stock market under a stock symbol. A real estate investment trust is set up to be entirely different from an average business. The investment trust is literally set up to generate income from the investment. This income is paid out in the form of dividends, and allows investors to diversify their risk by owning small pieces of multiple properties.

What You Are Supposed To Know About Real Estate

Most people actually confuse the term real estate with real estate business. The term real estate is not at all related to business, rather the term real estate is used as a term to represent a specific piece of property, land, or a combination of both. In most cases real estate also consists of the natural resources, parks, pools, and anything else that is attached to the land and is considered immovable. Real estate business, on the other hand, is the profession of selling, buying, or renting these properties.

There are many ways to get into the real estate business. By far the most common is becoming a real estate agent. Real estate agents are tasked with the difficult job of matching the needs of a buyer and a seller. A good real estate agent is familiar with the locality, so that they can properly assist with any increase or decrease in property values. For example, a good real estate agent should be able to tell you about any planned building that may increase the price of nearby properties. Also, a good agent should be able to recommend any improvements that could enhance prices. Whatever you do, do not take the agents word for anything. Make sure they can show you comparable properties within the geographic area and the sales prices those properties have received.

Things To Remember About Real Estate Agents

As a general rule, most real estate agents are usually very nice and upfront about things. There are however, a couple things that you should be concerned about. For starters, real estate agents are not legally bound to show you the best properties, or tell you all the things they know about the property. If they are asked a direct question, they cannot lie. But it is not in their best interest to point out any flaws that you did not see. Also, real estate agents may not disclose the behind the scenes they are working with another agent to sell a specific property. In order to protect yourself, make sure that the agent gives you access to the MLS listings. This will allow you to look at all the properties available on the market.

The real estate business is changing quickly. Today, the duty of an agent has almost been obliterated by online sites. Both buyers and sellers now have the ability to contact each other directly and choose the deals that fit their specific interests. This has allowed for increased transparency between both parties. There is one big caveat however, pictures online can often be misleading.

Tips About Real Estate

Investing in real estate can be a very profitable venture. However, in order to ensure your success, you must know what you are doing.

If you remember back to Chapter 3, I gave you the four rules of investing in real estate. As a refresher, they are:

The 4 Rules of Investing in Real Estate

1. Cash Flow

2. Buy Below Market

3. Use Leverage Correctly

4. Take Every Tax Advantage

At this point I would like to offer some additional tips that could help you become a great real estate investor. Remember, more than anything it is your job to make sure that you are purchasing a smart investment. At this point in the book, you should be comfortable making this decision.

Tip #1: Make Sure You Know The Market

Prior to investing any money in real estate, you should be able to gather enough information so that you understand the general market conditions. There are a literal ton of resources available to you. Make sure you take the time to read all the information you can get your hands on. You can never be too informed about your current market.

Make sure you pick an area that you know well. You will have much more success by focusing on a single market segment as opposed to taking on a variety of projects. It is very important that you stay within your comfort zone and use your knowledge of a certain geographic area. This will help ensure your success.

Tip #2: Focus On A Specific Type Of Real Estate

Long before you invest a single dollar of your money, decide which type of real estate you would like to invest in. Furthermore, have a plan for what you're going to do with the property. Are you going to be a house flipper? Are you going to be a landlord? Are you looking for rehab projects? Take the time to consider your skills and how comfortable you are managing each project.

Tip #3: Don't Assume Property Values Will Rise

As we have previously discussed, you now know that property values rarely outpace inflation. Don't ever make any financial assumptions that the property value is going to rise over time. Instead, you will want to focus on properties that can provide you with cash flow. This is why cash flow is the number one rule of investing in real estate.

Use extra caution when selecting tenants that will rent your property. The tenant should be able to comfortably afford the rent and the deposit. How else are they going to pay to live there?

Tip #4: Use All Your Resources

Take the time to search the market for foreclosures, as these can offer you the best opportunity to make more income. Foreclosure properties will be listed well below the market value of the house. There will always be heavy bidding and a lot of competitors, but if you win a foreclosure auction you could be sitting on a potential gold mine.

Additionally, be sure to ask your real estate agent to keep their ear out for any opportunities. Listen for opportunities to buy homes before they even hit the market. Consider any and all possibilities so that you don't miss out on a great deal.

The Keys To Making Real Estate Investing Profitable

People get confused about the real estate business. They frequently have bad information, and believe that real estate investing is more or less profitable as compared to some other business opportunities. Aside from the potential for yielding significant profits, either monthly or when you flip a property, investing in real estate can offer some really unique opportunities. Below are some ideas that could help make your investment more profitable.

1. Refurbish Real Estate To Increase Its Value

In the previous chapter, we talked about buying a stock, holding it for a period of time, and then reselling it for a profit. The profitability of that specific stock largely depends on the company's management, and their success. Unlike other investment instruments, real estate is directly under your control. Even though you cannot control changes that may occur in certain economic conditions, there are many other aspects that you can control to boost the returns on your investment. For example, fixing any repairs that are needed on the property or enhancing the property may increase its value. If you refurbish real estate correctly, the value of your investment will far outpace inflation and result in increased wealth for you.

2. Real Estate Investing Is Proven To Be Profitable Even During Economic Hardships

A good number of investors will state that during economic downturns, they are not sure of any places to invest their money. Most of these investors are tied to the stock market, and when the stock market is falling, they need somewhere else to invest their money. One thing that is important to remember is that people must live somewhere. No one has to own a stock.

3. Real Estate Is Not Affected By Inflation

As we have previously discussed, investing your money in real estate can protect you from the harsh effects of inflation. Because the value of real estate will rise over time, rental rates go upward along with property values and the cost of living. This is the nature of real estate. Owners are given the advantage of being able to adjust the rental rates to match the current economic conditions. This allows you to bring in more money as the property value rises and inflation decreases the value of a dollar.

4. Real Estate Investing Allows You To Use OPM

OPM, or other people's money, is often used in order to fund real estate deals. This is made possible because real estate is a physical property, and is called a hard asset. People with money to invest have the security of knowing that a physical property is being used as collateral.

One of the other reasons that real estate can be bought with debt is because it is considered less risky to the lender. By taking out a mortgage on the property, the lender or bank is literally handing you money to create a small business. While it does require some money to get into real estate, it does not require a lot of money to succeed in real estate.

5. Always Look Into The History Of The Property

As a new owner of a property, the last thing you want to have happen is to stumble upon some structural issue or some other major problem. It is important to always check the background, capability, and reputation of the company that constructed the property. If it is a fairly new property, make sure the developer has a good reputation about the properties they have built. If it is an older property, make sure to have a detailed inspection done.

6. Buy Property In Popular Areas

When considering purchasing a new property, keep in mind that the single most important factor is its location. Most real estate investors will tell you that it is a good idea to buy a property in an area that is improving not declining. Areas that are in decline will have a harder time filling tenant vacancies. You never want to be at risk of being unable to pay the bills because you can't find good tenants.

7. Make Sure You Have Enough Cash

If you are investing in a property, make sure that you have enough cash reserves on hand. Failure to have sufficient cash reserves can get you in multiple complicated situations. As a property owner, you must keep in mind that a lot of unexpected issues and emergencies will arise. As the owner, you need to have a reserve fund that is large enough to cater to these unforeseen emergencies.

Using real estate to increase your wealth

Think of someone you know who seems to have a great deal of money. You probably know that that person has invested in at least one property in order to increase their wealth. While they may not own more than just their own home, buying your personal house properly can increase your wealth long-term as well.

It is imperative that you remember that location has everything to do with real estate that is going to work out financially for us. Whether it be a new real estate development in the heart of the city, or a luxury high-rise with top-of-the-line amenities, you want to make sure that you are purchasing a valuable asset that you can rent out as a way to earn additional income.

It is important that your real estate be centrally located around some of the more popular locations in the area. It should be close to popular highways, so that commuters would consider your property. Also consider popular school districts, colleges and universities, parks, and convenience to work locations as well.

As we mentioned previously, no matter whether you are just trying to earn some extra income, or you want to seriously build wealth and move up in your lifestyle, investing in real estate is an excellent idea. You must do your research though, because not all real estate is desirable to renters. If you can't get good reliable tenants, then you are going to have a difficult time renting out the property. By picking something that is centrally located and has amenities that renters will love, you are ensuring that your property will stay rented most of the time. Additionally, you should frequently check with real estate agents to see what the going rental rates are in your geographic area. You may be pleasantly surprised to find that your property should rent for more money than it has prior.

Business Loans

Small Business Administration loans, or SBA loans for short, are loans that are given to small businesses which are not able to qualify for traditional bank loans. The reasons for non-qualification are various and range from lack of business history to lack of collateral. The SBA is not a direct lender, but it acts as an underwriter on behalf of the bank that is willing to fund the loans for the business entity. Should the borrower refuse to pay the loan, the SBA steps in, and pays the bank a percentage of the balance for taking the financial risk to give the funds to the business in the first place. There are multiple types of SBA loans.

Setting up your business is never going to be easy. There are a lot of details that need to be taken care of prior to even starting up. A lot of startup businesses are dependent on loans for every one of their business needs. It is therefore important to find an appropriate and reliable lending source to cater to your financial needs. However, since most conventional lenders and banks are not interested in providing loans to new business owners, a SBA loan may be an excellent idea to help get your dream off the ground.

Small businesses contribute greatly in enhancing our nation's economy. The Small Business Administration is a United States government agency that generates and gives loans to small businesses with the aim of improving the country's overall financial condition. These loans are meant to support small businesses by providing adequate financial assistance. Loans are not received directly from the SBA, but rather through a number of their lending partners that work with the SBA.

SBA loans are usually given to business owners at reduced interest rates compared to traditional loans. This is due to the fact that most startup business owners do not have enough capital in order to start their business without these loans.

SBA loans are provided to the business owners under an SBA guarantee. This guarantee makes sure that the loan is repaid on time to the lending partner. In most instances, you can obtain a SBA loan very fast with fewer hurdles than traditional financing. These loans are immensely beneficial for startup businesses that need financial assistance quickly.

One of the many beneficial aspects of an SBA loan is that they can be approved even if you have a poor credit score. Some people have gotten SBA loans even after declaring bankruptcy.

While it is not the intent of this book to go into all the different SBA loans, they do offer many different types including loans for real estate, equipment, disaster loans, and microloans.

Now it is time to spend a few minutes talking about some of the more conventional business loans available.

Conventional Business Loans

Conventional business loans are usually unsecured funds. This means that there is not an asset used as collateral in order to approve the loan. Conventional business loans are usually reserved for business entities that have good banking relationships and an established credit history. Conventional business loans can be written in a variety of ways, including balloon loans, or more traditional loans with monthly payments.

Equipment Leasing

Equipment leasing is a financial instrument which is not technically a loan. Leases are typically handled by large corporations or banks. Lease terms will vary, and usually range from 1 to 10 years. There are specific tax benefits to the business entity that leases the equipment.

Equipment Sale Leaseback

An equipment sale leaseback is a business loan that uses equipment as collateral in order to secure funds for the present needs of the business. The term of repayment will vary, and the amount of funds that can be secured will also vary widely as well.

Some people find this term confusing. The easiest way to think about this is that a company had to purchase equipment at some time in the past. Let's say the company now has an opportunity to do something else but needs a lot of capital in order to make it happen.

In this example, the company would pledge the equipment as collateral for a loan. The same company that pledges the equipment as collateral for the loan then leases the equipment back at a monthly rate. This allows the company to use the equipment while securing a large amount of capital for present business conditions or expansion opportunities. Many companies lease as opposed to buying equipment out right. This allows large amounts of capital to be preserved for future business opportunities.

Merchant Cash Advances

Merchant cash advances are used by businesses that need quick cash and do not qualify or do not have the time to go through the process of getting a traditional bank loan. A merchant cash advance is also not a typical loan. In reality, it is selling the assets of credit card receipts at a discount. In other words, a merchant cash advance company buys the credit card receipts of the business at a discount. Every time the business then "batches" or settles the day's business, they pay a fee until all the advanced funds are paid off. There is no set term or duration with a merchant cash advance.

Accounts Receivable Factoring

Accounts receivable factoring is not technically a loan either, but is actually selling invoices that you have billed at a discount for quick cash. In most transactions, the company invoicing the bills to other companies applies with a factoring company, and based on the quality of the accounts receivable, the invoices are purchased and funds are disbursed to the business within days. The dollar amount that is advanced can vary from between 50% to 90% of the invoice depending on various factors such as the size of the invoice, credit of the company being invoiced, and whether or not it is a company or government entity.

Medical accounts factoring is similar to the accounts receivable factoring, except for they favor medical entities. Medical factoring allows companies to sell their invoices for cash. In most cases, the health care industry must wait to receive payments from third parties like insurance companies, Medicaid, and Medicare. In the case of medical factoring, the medical facility would sell the invoices on an ongoing basis or all at one time.

Contract And Purchase Order Funding

Contract and purchase order funding allows companies to bid on large projects for governmental agencies, hospitals, universities, prison systems, and municipalities. It also allows small businesses to sell to larger corporations even if the business does not have the credit or bank approval to service or fulfill large orders. Similar to factoring, contract and purchase order funding is not a loan but rather a simultaneous transaction that involves advancing funds based on the credit of the governmental agency or the larger company and the size of the contract. Funds are advanced to the smaller company for the cost of finishing the order. The profit that would be gained is not advanced, but the costs such as raw materials, transportation, production, labor, and any other costs involved in completing the order are. Once the contract is completed, and an invoice is ready to be sent to the client, a factoring company usually steps in and buys the invoice at a discount so that the smaller company gets a portion of its profits immediately. By using contract and purchase order funding, smaller companies that are usually locked out of the bidding on large contracts can now be players on multi-million dollar deals.

Commercial Real Estate Sale Leaseback

Commercial real estate sales leasebacks work similar to the equipment sale leasebacks previously mentioned. Instead of utilizing equipment as collateral to secure cash, a piece of commercial real estate is used to gain access to funding. Any type of commercial real estate could be used, ranging from office buildings to medical buildings to franchises and even industrial buildings or large manufacturing facilities. This allows the company to free up capital that would have been tied up in real estate otherwise. Many companies can use the cash in order to grow their business faster. For example, a retailer selling goods may decide to focus on their retail operations, and lease the space because that real estate does not factor into their long term business plans.

Yes, the ownership of commercial real estate is an asset and can be used as collateral for a loan, but it may not always meet the needs of the business long term. An example of this is occurs if the business can add more locations and needs cash in order to finance the new inventory. Commercial real estate sale leasebacks are another form of gaining access to funds that has increased over the years.

As mentioned previously, business loans can be considered good debt. Often, a business loan can provide financial relief for different businesses. It is often critical for business owners to get additional funding in order to grow their business. When you are considering taking out a loan for your business, you must use a disciplined approach. I said it previously, and it bears repeating. You should only borrow money when you can legitimately make more profit dollars for your business. A ratio of 2 to 3 times profit dollars versus loan payment amount is a very safe calculation.

Business Plans

If you are considering applying for a business loan, it is important for you to remember that you must have a detailed and convincing business plan to present to a lender. Your business plan should include all relevant information that will help a lender provide you with the right type of financing for your company. Here is some basic information you should always include in your business plan.

1. Business structure
2. Purpose and goals of the business
3. Past success and future plans
4. Profit and loss projections
5. Cash flow projections that forecast repayment
6. Marketing and sales strategy
7. Specific purpose for funds

Things To Discuss With Your Lender

1. The amount of the loan required
2. Loan term or length

3. Interest rate and repayment schedule
4. Fixed or variable interest rate
5. Any additional fees or expenses
6. Loan collateral
7. Personal guarantee

CHAPTER 9
PASSIVE INCOME AND RETIREMENT

At this point in the book, we have talked about all the important things that you have to do in order to acquire wealth. We have spent a great deal of time talking about millionaires, and what their keys to success were. If you remember back to an earlier section of this book, we talked about the key to wealth creation being excelling at work, having a small business and smart investments in both real estate and equities.

If you really want to thrive in your retirement, you must also have a plan to maximize all the benefits you're going to receive once you quit actively working. We have already mapped out why I believe opening a small business is paramount to your success. At this point, we have also mapped out rental real estate and investing in equities. I believe the two previous chapters should have given you a basic general approach to starting in the stock market and with rental real estate.

In order to maximize all your financial benefits in retirement, we could not possibly introduce the world of finance without talking about passive income for a bit. Your road to wealth and financial freedom has to include passive income for your retirement.

Passive income is often considered to be the holy grail of investing. For multiple reasons, passive income is one of the keys to long term wealth creation and financial freedom. The major benefit of passive income is that income is generated regardless of the physical amount of work that you do.

Let's really think this concept through for a moment. How many hours can you physically work in one day? At a certain point there is a finite limit to the amount of time and effort that you can put into anything.

If you really want to begin using your earned money to make more money for you than you have to understand the concept of passive income. Income that is generated without you physically being present is one of the things that rich people are taught, or have learned over time. Ask yourself why we spent so much time talking about investments in rental real estate and equities for example.

In America, the lower and middle-class work really hard for their money. Those that have earned money in vast quantities understand the concept of putting their earned money to work for them in different ways. Imagine for a moment sitting at home and making five dollars per hour while you do whatever you want. Sounds like a pretty good deal right?

Now take this simple concept of sitting at home and scale it into a much larger idea. What if you could write a book or create a program that people would would buy day after day? Maybe you could create a phone app for instance?

In the United States, the Internal Revenue Service categorizes income into three broad categories. Those three categories are earned income, passive income, and portfolio income. Any and all money that you will make in your lifetime falls into one of these three categories.

As I mentioned previously, there is a finite amount of time every day. You could physically work every hour of every day without eating or sleeping, and there is still a cap in the amount of income that you could earn. This is what is referred to as earned income. In other words, you have to be there for income to be earned.

We have previously talked about dividends and capital gains, or profits, from the stock market. This is called portfolio income. Think about replacing your income for a moment. How much income would you need to produce from your portfolio? $50,000 per year? $80,000? More?

In order to make enough income from your investment portfolio to live on, you would need a large amount of capital working for you. For example, let's assume that you could safely expect to make 5% per year on your money. It would require $1 million in capital, making a 5% return per year, in order to generate $50,000 worth of income. No one that has $1 million in their investment portfolio should be reading a book entitled, Start Winning With Money.

As far as I know there are only two ways to generate passive income. The first method, is to have a large amount of money already. It should be fairly easy to make more money when you have a large amount already in your bank account. The second method of creating a passive income, is to invest your time and energy into creating something that will generate income whether you are actively working or not.

As you get closer towards retirement, it is important that a portion of your income is no longer generated by actively working. Here in the United States, people expect to live during their retirement by using a combination of funds from Social Security, retirement accounts (401k), and possibly a small pension. The problem with relying on only those three sources of income is that you cannot grow any one of them over time. Social security benefits and pensions are set at a fixed amount of income per month. Your retirement account has a limited amount of money in it.

In order for us to thrive during our golden years, we need to have sources of passive income. So the next logical question then is, how do we generate passive income?

The main reason that people find it difficult to transition from a lifestyle of earned income to passive income, is that our entire education system is actually teaching us to go out and get a job. I talked about this earlier in the book. As a child, you were also most likely taught that the amount of physical time you put into a job directly impacted the amount of money earned. It is not easy to unlearn these basic concepts that were ingrained at a young age.

I am not going to spend any time on how to generate passive income if you have the ability to make a large financial investment. While I still believe it is best to use your funds to invest in real estate and equities, there are many more books that cover this in intimate detail. I want to spend some time talking to the real people in America. The people that don't have $1 million in their bank account and genuinely need to change their financial focus.

For those of us that have had to, or are trying to, rebuild our financial future, we don't have a large pile of cash to spend on multiple investment ideas. Therefore, we need our business, and our investments, to generate income for us over time. Please remember that if you must physically be involved with your business in order to generate income, then it is not passive income. Examples of passive income business types include rental real estate, car washes, vending machines, laundromats, and storage units. You can also build your small business to run without your day to day involvement. Your income would then become passive.

On the personal side of things, if you are going to generate passive income you must do so through royalties and commissions. If you are a creative person, you should have the ability to sell photographs, write a book, or create a song. Whenever one of these items is purchased you then generate a royalty. If you are more technologically advanced, you may decide to create a website or an app that generates income from ad sales or affiliate marketing.

It is not my intent at this time to go into the details of passive income. I am really just trying to introduce the concept so that you can begin to understand its importance in your financial future. More than ever, the Internet is breaking down the barriers of traditional publishing and music creation. Ideally, if you are a creative person, then your small business will focus on generating revenue by utilizing one of these methods.

This book is a perfect example of passive income by the way. My small company, Masters Investment Group, is the publisher for all my books. Whenever someone purchases a book, the royalty is deposited into my business checking account. My business also generates income from ads on my website, traditional paperback book sales, and commissions earned from affiliate sales. None of these income sources require me to be physically present in order to be earned.

If you are a technological person, then your business should focus on creating a website or app that sells a physical or digital product. No matter what you sell it is important to remember that this income is generated whether you are physically working or not.

The greatest thing about passive income is that it can be scaled infinitely. What I mean by this is that I could sell one book this week and 10,000 books per week in 10 years time. The amount of work that you put into selling and promoting the book is the same either way. Most of your well known authors and musical artists continue to generate income from books or songs that were written years and years ago.

I believe it is also important to remember that in the age of the Internet, almost everyone is an expert in something. One of the most beautiful things about the Internet is that you can share information in real time. An example of this is trying to fix your car. You can literally watch a video and in most cases do the repair yourself in real time. At that specific moment, whoever created the video that you watched was an expert in that field. As crazy as that probably sounds, someone, somewhere, is an expert on repairing a 1978 Ford Pinto.

Below I have listed the Top 7 Sources of Passive Income. These are from an article I wrote on my blog some time ago, but they have not changed. All of these are time tested ways to make income passively.

The Top 7 Sources of Passive Income

1. Rental real estate

2. e-Books

3. Advertising

4. Affiliate links

5. Apps

6. Dividends

7. Buy an existing business

As it pertains to real estate, rental real estate is the number one source of passive income for a lot of people. If managed properly, rental real estate can require next to zero time and effort. You can actually outsource the entire process of finding tenants for example. You can even hire a property manager to schedule and assist with all the repairs, collect rent checks, find new tenants, and evict bad tenants for you.

The reason that rental real estate tops our list is that so many people use it as a foundation for their business. Remember, we have already proven that 90% of millionaires own real estate, even if it is just their primary residence. With all of that money, why wouldn't you just rent a beautiful place so you didn't have to deal with repairs and maintenance of a home?

The reason that millionaires own real estate, even if it's only their own property, is because they know it is a better investment than just throwing your money away on renting something. There is nothing wrong with renting a property short term, but if you are truly going to build wealth then you are going to have to purchase real estate at some point. Ideally, rental real estate is a piece of your portfolio going forward.

E-Books are changing how the world shares information. Odds are, you're reading one right now. With the advent of the Internet came the ability to share large amounts of data with very little buffer between the creator and the end user. Just as Apple and iTunes did to music, so has Amazon and Barnes & Noble done to reading. The average person is now able to consume a lot more content at a much more reasonable price by utilizing e-books.

What you probably didn't know however, is that e-books

offer a source of passive income for years and years. As an example of this, my first book, <u>Mattress Buying 101</u>, is now on it's second electronic edition. This book continues to generate royalties every month. As long as the book is available for sale, and the content is still relevant to the end user, it will produce income for years to come.

Advertising and affiliate links tend to go hand in hand with a website. As part of the process of opening a business, you will most likely need a website in order to help spread your brand awareness. Once you have established a website, you can begin to offer advertising to other companies and create income from affiliate links.

Remember that expert on the 1978 Ford Pinto? Once that person helps you fix your problem, then they have the right to ask you to help support them. One of the ways that the average person can ask you to help support them for their advice is now affiliate links. An example of this is the repair video using a certain brand of tool. The person in the video could have a relationship with the tool company, and provide you a link to go to their website. Once you click on that link, you make a purchase, and the company credits the original advertiser for the getting that sale. Usually the dollar amounts are not very large. In most cases, affiliate links tend to earn less than $10. But remember one very important thing. Affiliate links can be scaled infinitely. Should that video, or more likely a series of videos, become highly popular then you can expect many more clicks through the affiliate link. In the Internet world, more clicks equals more income.

With more clicks, and more eyes on your website, you can also begin to sell advertising to other businesses. Traditional advertising was sold on the number of subscribers. This applied to newspapers and magazines, as well as television viewers. In the Internet world, advertising prices are based on the number of eyeballs that will see it. Prominent locations on high-traffic websites can be extremely lucrative. Think about one of your favorite websites for example. How much do you think the company could charge for an ad that sits on their home page for an entire day? I can assure you that based on the number of people that would see the advertisement, the price is in the thousands.

On the mobile side of things, applications, or apps for short, have become highly lucrative inventions. Large companies are spending a lot of money to develop apps because the return on their investment can be astronomically high. For example, in doing some research for my blog about this specific topic, I found out that the app Flappy Bird was making more than $50,000 per day in revenue at it's peak in popularity.

In fact, some companies prize their position on your cellular phone. Large companies are even willing to give away highly profitable apps for free, just so they know you will use the app, and contribute to their revenue streams.

Companies are also creating apps so they can gain insight to the consumer. Companies can use apps to introduce new products for example. They can also make you watch an ad for a reward in a game. A lot of times when you sign up for a game you also attach your Facebook page. The company then gains insight into what you look at and what you're interested in.

Make no mistake, apps have become a big business. If you are technologically savvy, this may be an avenue that you want to explore for your own small business purposes.

The final two sources of passive income, dividends and buying an existing business, are more traditional streams of revenue. Dividends have existed for years. If you were to ask the older generation, I'm sure they would willingly share some information about the days when savings accounts, certificates of deposit, and stocks and bonds paid great dividends. While this more traditional method of passive income seems to be under attack in recent years, there are some highly reputable companies that pay a consistent, and reliable dividend.

Buying an existing business also offers a more traditional revenue stream. I do have to make one thing really clear right now. In order for your investment dollars to truly be passive income, you cannot work in the business. Remember, working a day to day job is earned income, not passive income.

Examples of passive income businesses are vending machines, ATM machines, coin-operated laundry, storage facilities, real estate businesses, and restaurants with a dedicated management team.

The business itself may require some very active members of management, but in order for your investment to be considered passive, you may not personally work in the business. Whatever choices you make. Please remember our only rule; if you have to physically work in the business, then it is not passive income.

CHAPTER 10
START WINNING WITH MONEY

I would like to take the time to thank you for purchasing my book. By the time you're reading this sentence, I will have spent more than 12 months writing, rewriting, and editing these pages. Before we end this journey together, I wanted to take a few moments and share some of my most important life lessons.

If you remember the early pages of this book, I explained to you what my personal key to true wealth was. In case you don't remember, it sounded like this.

"I personally believe the key to true wealth is a simple formula that involves a combination of work, timing, and knowledge. No one achieves greatness without all three of these factors. Please do not confuse wealth with money. All the money in the world can not make you wealthy. Wealth can not be bought. It is achieved."

True wealth is a mindset. It is not something that can be bought, nor is it something that can be defined by a bank balance. The size of your bank account is no indication of where you are in your life as it pertains to achieving true wealth. As I said in the very beginning of this book, I know many people in life that do not have a large bank account but are extremely wealthy.

I want to take the time to caution those individuals that look at money as anything more than a scorecard. Your bank account balance, no matter how large or small, is nothing more than a scorecard to tell you where you are in your journey.

Think about the best teacher you ever had for a moment. No matter the subject, that teacher was able to bring you into a world that you had very little education in. That same teacher was then able to teach you the subject, craft your understanding of the subject, and make sure that you were at a satisfactory level of understanding so that you would then be able to teach the subject.

Your financial scorecard should be looked at the same way. For example, having a small bank balance does not make you any less of a person. The scorecard, or bank balance, is simply telling you that you haven't spent enough time learning the subject at hand. On the other side of the equation, once you have achieved a large bank balance, the scorecard is now telling you that you have achieved a satisfactory level of understanding and that you should be able to teach the subject.

I sincerely hope that you will assist me in educating the next generation. I have openly shared my concerns with the public school system, as well as the lack of financial education being taught in the United States today. I am not sure how we can ever expect someone to do well when we do not give them the tools to succeed.

Start Winning With Money is a dream of mine. For me it's a dream that we can slowly educate our children about financial matters. I can assure you they are not getting a financial education in the public school system. In most cases, they are not getting a financial education in the private school system. Time after time we have seen students leave high school and college with almost zero preparation to handle their personal finances.

Ultimately it is up to you and I to combat the financial failures of this country's educational system. In my opinion, the best way to do that is from home. Once you have mastered your own personal financial situation, then you can speak openly from a position of love, understanding, and patience. Openly share your passion for people doing well in life. Be proud of your successes and failures.

As for me and my family, our definition of true wealth is the perfect balance between love, family, friends, money, and time. I personally do not believe that anyone can achieve true wealth without having all of these five factors balanced in their life. Many people can balance three or even four of these aspects at one time, but to balance all five is the ultimate goal.

As it pertains to love, I am not merely talking about love for your current partner or spouse. I am not talking about love for your children. I am talking about love in a much larger context. To me the true definition of love is wanting to promote the best of someone else and watching them succeed beyond your wildest dreams. As a parent, I can think of no better indication of success than to watch my child exceed their every expectation.

In an even broader sense, try to promote love to the world. It is very easy to partake in a culture where we tear other people down for achieving success. I do not understand this mindset. It is perfectly natural to be jealous of someone for achieving financial success. What is not natural however, is wasting all your precious time and energy on hatred and jealousy. It takes just as much time to show hate as it does to show love. Additionally, all the time spent trying to tear down someone else is time you could have spent trying to build up your own family.

When talking about friends and family, I want to be sure that you understand the need for support from both. Families can be a very tricky dynamic. Do not ever allow someone in your family to dictate your happiness or success in life. Choose your friends carefully, and your real close personal friends even more carefully. Make sure that both your family and friends help you to become a better person in all aspects of life. The single most important piece of advice I can give someone is this, if you want to be better then you are in any aspect of life, surround yourself with people that can help to get there.

I hope that this book has taught you the basics of money

management and financial freedom. I attempted to write a book that combined all the best financial advice I had received over the years no matter the format it was presented in. I have read Dave Ramsey, Robert Kiyosaki, Clark Howard, Tony Robbins and many many more. I believe that they all have a message that is worth reading. I would not list their books on my website if I did not believe they were worth taking the time to read. I have done my best to combine certain aspects of all their teachings. I have added my own personal thoughts as well. By now you should be a fine tuned machine as it pertains to personal finance, starting a small business, and investments.

Time is the one thing we can never get back. No matter how much financial success you achieve, you can never go back and replay your life. Time truly stops for no one. Once one's journey to true wealth has been achieved, and the other four factors have aligned in harmony, you can begin to focus on slowly leaving your daily routine behind. You should begin to put other people in place that can continue to promote your business goals. You should be able to walk away from a full time job and let your business blossom. You should have a healthy combination of investments that are creating a passive income. The combination of all these successful techniques will allow you to create more time in your life to do the things you want to do. I personally suggest that you heavily consider spending more time with friends and family, as well as leaving a lasting legacy on the world. I'm not suggesting everyone write a book or complete projects just to do something. I am suggesting that you work with someone or something you are passionate about and commit your time and effort to making the world a better place when you leave it. For me personally it's about writing books and hoping that my words can inspire someone to do great things long after I am gone.

I sincerely hope that having spent some time reading this book you now also understand why I entitled the book, Start Winning With Money. It was never my intent to write page after page of specific information that only applies to each unique situation. My goal was to write a more general guideline that would help the average person make basic financial decisions without having to become an expert on finance.

I believe we have a financial epidemic in this country. So many people in the United States have been, and currently are mismanaging their finances. Your finances directly impact your life and the choices that you can make at any given time. While money is not the end all be all, it is vitally important to understand that money will dictate your options.

I continue to be amazed when people tell me they do not have the time to think about their finances. Many people I have conversations with have openly admitted that they don't understand their 401(k) plan. It amazes me that we can always find 30 minutes to play on our cell phone, but never 30 minutes to focus on our budget. As with anything in life, maybe it is easier to pretend that it's not a problem, as opposed to having to deal with the problem.

There's an old expression in the writing world that in order to write a successful book you must write about something you know about. I promise to you that I know about broke. I know about being broke, unemployed, and worrying about having to pay bills. I know what it feels like to lose a home to foreclosure. I know about bad money decisions, and the impact that they have on relationships. I have openly shared my experiences from a position of love, understanding, and patience.

In the beginning of the book I openly shared that I'm not wealthy by the traditional means of measurement. I am not a millionaire. I am however truly wealthy. I am beyond blessed to have true love in my life. I have a friend, partner, and spouse that fully supports the decisions I make. I genuinely offer love to the world, and try to make people better for knowing me. I have family and friends that support my dreams. At this point in my life, I have enough money to be comfortable. I have an emergency fund. The only part of the equation that I can never seem to find enough of is time. But please do not misunderstand me when I say this. I am telling you that I can never find enough time because I still have a lot of things I would like to do. I am blessed that I no longer have to do anything I don't want to.

I want you to start winning with money. The reason that I wrote this book in the style and order that I did it, was for two different reasons. First, I needed to write text that was fun to read. Second, I needed to provide real world examples and documentation that proved there is a better way to live.

I specifically chose the order of the chapters in an attempt to prove that I understand and I have made the same mistakes in the past. I wish someone would have sat down with me at the age of 18 and had a hard conversation about the real world. I needed to hear the hard truths about earning money, spending money, and going into debt. I wish someone would have defined good debt and bad debt for me. I wish someone would have sat down and explained the financial consequences of our decisions while teaching me about the four downright lies that are being fed to the American consumer everyday.

Once that conversation was over, I would have been willing to listen to the reality of life. You can decide to go to college and get an education. You can literally go hundreds of thousands of dollars in debt in order to achieve that goal. I also would have been willing to listen to the other side of the equation. Someone should have told me that not going to college and starting your own small business is an option. There are many HVAC technicians, plumbers, electricians, and contractors that have hardly any post secondary education. They are trained in an in-demand trade. They have satisfying careers and make really good money. Many of these tradesmen have grown their business beyond their wildest dreams.

After having made the decision between going to college or starting my own small business, I would have wanted someone to sit down with me and explain the basics of sales. That is why that chapter came next.

The second half of the book was then written from the angle that your life has probably gone something like mine. You have probably made a lot of mistakes in your life. There are a lot of things you probably would have liked to have done differently. That's perfectly OK. We're all human. We have all made the same mistakes. That is why I thought it was so important to write a chapter about taking the time to reset your life. You have to draw the line somewhere. We live in a wonderful country that allows us to make the decision to continue doing the same things we've always done. You can continue spending money on credit cards. You can continue to rack up debt. Or you can make the conscious choice to make a decision today to change your life.

Once you have made a decision that you should change your life, the next chapters of the book had to be written about successful things you can do to change your financial situation. It only makes sense to look at the basics of investing in connection to making future financial gains. Not everyone who invests in real estate is a millionaire, and that's OK. You may not be the next Warren Buffet as it pertains to the stock market either, and that's also OK. Investing in both real estate and stocks will change your financial future for the better.

And lastly, once you have accepted the fact that real estate and the stock market offers the best chance of changing your family's financial future, then we had to have a chapter about real estate and business loans. I'm not professing to be an expert on either subject. There are many, many books written on both subjects that can help you educate yourself when the time is right. Until you are ready to go to that next level, do not waste your time, effort, and energy on any activity that is not helping you get where you want to go. Always remember, you cannot out save inflation.

After all of that material was covered, I thought it was important to remind you that I am writing all of this in an effort to promote true wealth. I want more people to be wealthy beyond their wildest imagination. But the key to this is that you can obtain wealth in many aspects of life. I have outlined my five key wealth principles and shared them with you. Maybe you share my desire to fulfill your life. I hope there are several things that are important to you in life. As for me, there are several things that are important to me in life. One is that I tried to help other people succeed in life. I am a firm believer in one very basic business principle; take care of your customer, and do the right thing without fail. If you do the right thing without fail and you take care of the customer to your best ability, you will receive a financial windfall beyond your wildest dreams.

Remember the text that you are reading right this second was written by a guy they got his start by writing a mattress book. That small little book exceeded every expectation I ever had for it. Because of that one small step that I took several years ago, I am now expanding my customer base.

I also know about success in life. I am gainfully employed in a profession I like. I own my own small business that is growing every week. Masters Investment Group has multiple sources of passive income for my older years. I have investments in both real estate and the stock market currently. I am currently working on building my portfolio of passive income to allow me to retire with respect and dignity. I will not be a victim of the system. I will not rely on Social Security to fund my retirement.

Thank you for committing the time, effort, and energy to read my book. I had a school teacher remind me years ago that if you only got one great idea from a book then it was worth every page read. I hope you can say that at this point. I have had an absolute blast writing, rewriting, and proof reading this book. Working on this book has reminded me how truly wealthy I am. I hope someday soon that you can say that too.

I am a winner! You are a winner! We can all Start Winning With Money!

ABOUT THE AUTHOR

Donnie Masters is the current owner and president of Masters Investment Group. He is an accountant for a small private business, as well as an American book author. Donnie was born and raised in Martinsburg, West Virginia.

In 2015, after having spent more than 15 years as a restaurant manager and retail store manager, Donnie began working on his first book. Mattress Buying 101 was published in June 2016.

Mattress Buying 101 is a how-to book on properly buying a mattress. The book was written as a guide to help the average consumer purchase the best mattress for their budget. Donnie's inspiration for writing the book was based on his career at Sleepy's, where he rose from salesperson to district manager in just 3 years time.

After his first book's success in the small niche genre of mattresses, Donnie decided to write again on a couple more subjects he knew about, business and money. Start Winning With Money was started in September of 2016.

In early 2017, Donnie founded the Masters Investment Group and began focusing his energy on financial education. He continues to actively work as an accountant and write full time. For more information, please visit his website at:

www.DonnieMasters.com

Donnie can also be reached on Twitter and Facebook:

Twitter: @realdonniem

Facebook: www.facebook.com/realdonniemasters

Email: mastersinvestmentgroupllc@gmail.com

www.ingramcontent.com/pod-product-compliance
Lightning Source LLC
Chambersburg PA
CBHW051208170526
45166CB00013B/1912